d/2 3/6

Bookseller
NW

Whirlpool near Alt Breysach.

London, John W. Parker & Son, West Strand, 1854.

OUR CRUISE IN THE UNDINE:

THE JOURNAL

OF

AN ENGLISH PAIR-OAR EXPEDITION

THROUGH

FRANCE, BADEN, RHENISH BAVARIA, PRUSSIA, AND BELGIUM.

BY THE CAPTAIN.

The Etchings by One of Ourselves.

LONDON:
JOHN W. PARKER AND SON, WEST STRAND.
MDCCCLIV.

LONDON:
SAVILL AND EDWARDS, PRINTERS, CHANDOS STREET,
COVENT GARDEN.

CONTENTS.

Chapter I.

PAGE

INTRODUCTION 1

Chapter II.

OUTWARD BOUND.

Noms de voyage—A mistake—' Off she goes'—The baggage—
Rouen—We arrive at Paris 4

Chapter III.

PARIS AND THE SEINE.

Arrival of the Undine—The Paris boat club—Its constitution
and rules—Caution unheeded—A boating dinner at
Bougeval—Curiously shaped boat—Fairly started—Frogs
and bargees—The banks of the Seine—Montereau. . . 11

CONTENTS.

CHAPTER IV.

DIJON—LE CÔTE D'OR.

The Yonne—Disappearance of the Professor—Sens—St. Florentin—Canal inspectors—Tonnerre—Ladies bathing—Le Côte d'Or—Montbard—Dijon—A filly 24

CHAPTER V.

ST. JEAN DE L'OSNE.

Our reception—Dangerous position of the boat—Imagination of the natives—A dance—Dress of an English gentleman—We show off, and take our leave 33

CHAPTER VI.

BESANÇON—LE PETIT QUART D'HEURE.

The Canal du Rhône au Rhin—Dôle—A sanguinary bargee—The river Doubs—A tunnel—Rough quarters—Besançon—The Doctor in pawn—Railway officials 41

CHAPTER VII.

CHANGE FOR A NAPOLEON.

Locks and weirs—The Captain turns washerwoman—The scenery of the Doubs—Quaint lodgings—Primitive mode of washing—Small charges—Clerval—A race—The Captain in a mess—Chinese notions prevalent 51

Chapter VIII.

STORMS NEAR BASLE.

The Vosges Mountains—An attack—The boat is smashed—repairs necessary—The Mayor of Kembs—A triumphal procession—Advice unnoticed—Suspicious characters . 64

Chapter IX.

AM RHEIN.

Neumburg—The bridge at Alt Breysach—The Cornishman's drive—Great speed we attain—A critical position—We reach Strasburg—Civilized life not congenial—Lauterbourg—Plain sailing—A Sunday on the Rhine—Mannheim—Ship! Duck!—Tidings of the 'Water Lily' 76

Chapter X.

HEIDELBERG—A SCHLÄGER-FECHT.

Gentlemen—The Neckar—The Captain chucks pebbles—The Professor outwitted—Mine Host and his nephews—Visitors—Schläger-fechte—We witness a combat—a description thereof—Moral 90

Chapter XI.

MOSQUITOES AND WORMS.

The retreat—Guntersblum and its inhabitants—Mayence—Frankfort—The British Consul—Rudesheim—A wandering school—The Bingen Professor—Passage of the Bingen-loch 106

Chapter XII.

BINGEN TO COLOGNE.

Lorch—An echo—Louis-Philippe at the Lurlei-felsen—Boppard—Kilkenny cats—Stolzenfels—Coblentz—Neuwied—Königswinter and the Drachenfels—An attempted mutiny—The public press—Legend of Cologne Cathedral . . . 116

Chapter XIII.

BELGIUM—THE CUSTOM HOUSE.

Belgium—The Custom House—The rail—More newspapers—Ghent—The Béguinage—Plight of the boat—Douaniers and their notions—Bloemendael—Bruges—Le Prefecteur d'Arrondissement—Simplicity of the natives—We are summoned—Ostend 131

Chapter XIV.

Conclusion 146

ILLUSTRATIONS.

WHIRLPOOL NEAR ALT BREYSACH . . . *facing Title.*

MAP OF OUR ROUTE THROUGH FRANCE, GERMANY,

    WEST FLANDERS, ETC. . . . . *p.* 1

CANAL INSPECTORS 26

ARRIVAL AT ST. JEAN DE L'OSNE 34

ON THE BANKS OF THE DOUBS 44

SUSPICIOUS CHARACTERS 74

PASSING THE SHALLOWS 82

FERTIG! LOSS! 102

A WARM NIGHT NEAR GERNSHEIM 108

MAKING THE BEST OF IT 110

SHIP! DUCK! 126

OUR CRUISE IN THE UNDINE.

CHAPTER I.

INTRODUCTION.

Jaq. de Bois. Let me have audience for a word or two.
As You Like It.

ANOTHER! Why I thought there was a book about a pair-oar expedition published last year. Very true, gentle reader, and more than this, the year before brought into public life 'The Log of the Water Lily;' and the kind reception that these met with, has been one cause in the publication of the present journal.

It has been the writer's misfortune never to have seen the former of those books, and he was on the point of leaving England when the second, 'The Water Lily on the Danube,' was just put into his hands. He need not say how much he was gratified by a perusal of the work, for having spent

B

INTRODUCTION.

some time in England in a small boat, he had often wished to have been himself party to a more extensive voyage. His travels were confined merely to the canals, rivers, and small lakes of Cambridgeshire, and the neighbouring counties; a small craft, rigged schooner fashion, carried himself and man Friday, with double and single barrelled gun, dog and provisions, and also a tarpaulin covering, with horse rugs *ad lib.* to keep out the rain and night air. The scenery was not over interesting, to be sure, but there was a plenty of good shooting for the sportsman, for the ecclesiologist numerous fine churches to inspect, and for the lover of good cheer, a set of real English farmers, hearty and always glad to see one. Thus, to one of the crew of the 'Undine' at least, this mode of travelling was not altogether new.

Last May, two of our party having completed their peregrinations of Dartmoor, were visiting on foot the lovely and picturesque valleys, and the rugged cliff scenery of North Devon (intending thence to cross over into Wales, and so on to the Lakes) when one of them received a letter from the Professor, inviting him (if a third could be found to do the work of bow in a pair oar) to undertake a cruise through France, and down the

INTRODUCTION. 3

Rhine. Fortunately here was a third hand, who was willing to make up the crew, and immediately an answer was returned, accepting the offer, though leaving the Professor to strike out the course, and do all that was necessary in regard of the boat before starting.

In the following pages, the writer makes no attempt at flowing language, or even a description of the beauties of scenery ; they contain essentially what they profess to give—viz., a simple and un-varnished account of our cruise in the ' Undine.'

As regards the greater part of our route, ' volumes have been poured forth, and will be succeeded by volumes, as long as the noblest scenes of nature can excite admiration, or until some miracle rob men of the desire to tell what they have seen, and express what they feel.'

CHAPTER II.

OUTWARD BOUND.

'Ορμώμεθ' ἐς ναῦν, μηδ' ἐπίσχωμεν τὸ πλεῖν.
PHILOCTETES.

ON the 2nd of June we all three met by appointment in London, to arrange about our future proceedings.—The first thing we did was to adopt certain *noms de voyage,* though our passports, of course, carried our real names. One—the Professor, as we called him (though it was no easy matter to find a soubriquet for that distinguished personage), was to have the entire charge and management of the funds, the procuring of provisions, and in fact of everything in connexion with money matters. The Captain (a quondam Captain of his College Boat Club) was intrusted with the command and care of the boat; while the Doctor (the little Doctor, as he has always been called among his old associates), having never before crossed the Channel, was to be allowed more leisure than the others to look about him, but was also to keep a strict eye on the knapsacks, &c., when we arrived at any town, lest, perhaps, they might be carried off by some well-intentioned *commissionaire* or hotel porter; and a very good hand at this work he eventually proved to be, for whenever we were annoyed by one of those most troublesome of all creatures, we invariably set the Doctor to work at him; nor was he the less successful either in ridding us of this importunate race because his stock of French was limited.

We next visited the yard of Messrs. Noulton and Wyld, boatbuilders, Lambeth, with whom we had previously corresponded, and found that the boat would be ready to leave London the following morning. She was a new boat this season, of precisely the same make and build as the 'Water Lily,' which descended the Danube last year;

and the Captain, with the consent of his crew, determined on having her named 'The Undine.'

Passports were the next things to be procured; and as it is necessary to have a certificate to the fact of one's being a British subject, in making an application for a Foreign Office passport, a younger brother of the Captain's had been requested to obtain them for himself and the Doctor, from a magistrate of the town in which they resided. In making our application by letter for these passports, the Captain, by an oversight, enclosed his brother's letter instead of the note he himself had written, the which, had it by any chance happened to have fallen into Lord Clarendon's own hands, would have surprised him rather, especially since his Lordship's own name is George. It ran thus—

DEAR GEORGE,

I enclose the certificates you desired, and hope they are what you are in want of,

Yours ever,

T. H. H.

The following morning the Professor left with the boat for Newhaven, intending to proceed at once to Dieppe; while we were to complete our purchases in the shape of costume, and join him the next day, not forgetting to take with us a diminutive specimen of

> The flag that's braved a thousand years
> The battle and the breeze.

We reached Dieppe at ten o'clock in the evening, and having nothing but a knapsack each, we were not detained at the Custom House above five minutes.—Met the Professor, and were glad to learn from him that he had arranged everything about the boat, and that she had left that morning by the *petite vitesse*, or luggage train, and would probably arrive in Paris in two days' time.

It would be well, perhaps, for the good of posterity, to enumerate briefly the stock of clothing we each took with us. It consisted of a straw hat, a white neckerchief, an alpaca coat for towns, light waistcoat ditto, two shirts, two merino jerseys, one sky-blue flannel ditto, two pairs of flannel trowsers, two pairs of socks, four pocket handkerchiefs, a pair of canvas shoes, a comb and a tooth brush, and a mackintosh rolled up on the top of the knapsack; and beyond this the Doctor had furnished himself with a book or two—the Professor with his fishing rod and commissionaire's pouch, while the Captain took charge of the union jack, belonging to the boat.

We started for Rouen by rail, and *en route* caught a glimpse of the 'Undine' stowed away very carefully on some trucks of hay, while they lay at a small station allowing us to pass.

Arriving at Rouen we visited some of the principal *lions* of the place, more for the Doctor's sake than anything else, for both the Captain and Professor had seen the town before. It was only a few places, though, that we honoured with our presence, for we all had an objection to *doing* a town in the customary manner of Englishmen abroad—that is, of seeing the greatest number of things in the least possible time: and we were convinced moreover, that there is nothing so fatiguing as sight-seeing, especially in towns; not that this prevented our visiting what we conveniently could on our way. But, by the ordinary visitor to the fine old town of Rouen, at least a week should be devoted, for besides the numberless antiquities it possesses, and the venerable picturesqueness of most of the streets, it is unlike most other towns where such old buildings remain, in this, that it is a bustling place of business, and for this cause it has been often called the Manchester of France.

OUTWARD BOUND. 9

There is an excellent description of Rouen in
Murray's *Hand-book*, to which work I would refer
my curious reader for an account of this or any
other town I may mention; for it is not my object,
as I have above stated, to launch out into a minute
description of the places we pass, since in such a
mere journal as the present it would be wholly out
of place. The route from Dieppe to Paris especially needs little or no comment, seeing so many of
our own countrymen travel yearly over this railway, the greater part of which, by the bye, was
made by 'navvies' imported from England for
the purpose.

The lovely scenery on the banks of the winding
Seine, and the richness of the surrounding country,
would have delighted us much had we not been
pestered by a loquacious Englishman, who persisted in perpetrating what he considered to be
jokes. He told us that he was the tallest man
in existence, for that he *reached* the whole way
from Dover to Calais—a vile pun which the Doctor
declared ought to have been rewarded by an
emetic at least.

On our arrival in Paris, where we intended
stopping a few days, we took up our quarters in

the Rue St. Nicholas, and then called on Mr. J. Arthur, an English gentleman of whom Messrs. Noulton and Wyld had made mention to us, and who has had several English-built boats sent over to Paris, principally for the use of a boat club which he was attempting to form.

We were agreeably surprised at meeting with an attempt of this nature on the continent; and I believe that it will not be uninteresting to the readers of this little work, if, before entering upon its immediate subject, I devote two or three pages to a description of the novel experiment which the energy and experience of Mr. Arthur has already brought to so successful an issue.

CHAPTER III.

PARIS AND THE SEINE.

Ant.—The bark is ready,
My lord, and all prepared.
                Marino Faliero.

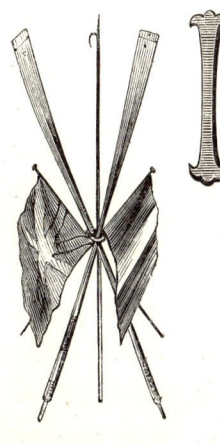

IN the morning Mr. Arthur accompanied us to the railway station to inquire for the boat,—and finding that she had arrived and was ready to leave the station, we hired a large covered cart, and getting into it, boat and all, started for Asnières, a small place at the junction of the Versailles and St. Germain's railroad, where Mr. Arthur kept his boats.

Our craft was the admiration of several members,

of the Paris boat club, concerning which it behoves me to say a few words.

Having witnessed the defeat of one or two very mild English boats on the Seine by some wretchedly bad French rowers, our friend conceived the idea of giving them a licking in return, being confident of success, on account of the utter ignorance of the art and mystery of pulling among the French.

Accordingly, he requested Messrs. Noulton and Wyld to send him a four-oared outrigger, and having manned her tolerably to his satisfaction, challenged the best eight-oared boat on the Seine. It is almost unnecessary to say that their efforts were crowned with success, for they were a plucky crew, and determined to win.

After this victory, several Englishmen residing in Paris wished to join the crew; this led Mr. Arthur to the establishment of a club consisting at the present moment of about twenty members, and possessing six or seven boats, with every prospect of being still stronger next season. Much interest has been shown in regard of their proceedings last summer, and they have won in all twenty-five prizes this season—not a bad start for a young club labouring under the disadvantages that such an one necessarily must encounter.

THE PARIS BOAT CLUB. 13

At present, however, they are under distinguished patronage. The right honourable Lord Cowley is the president, and the committee of management consists of *Captain*—Viscount A. Chateauvillard, Hon. W. Stuart, Mr. F. Ricardo, Mr. Lowe, *Hon. Sec.*—Mr. J. Arthur.

The rowing dress we, as Cambridge men, were glad to learn, is to consist of 'sky-blue jersey with short sleeves, white flannel trowsers, and straw hat with blue ribbon.' Among the rules of the club there is one which might profitably be imitated by some of our own boat clubs; it is this —' That the utmost harmony do for ever prevail in the Paris rowing club.' Great praise is due to the Honorary Secretary for his unremitting zeal in the establishment of the club, and the management of its affairs.

With great generosity, he speaks in high terms of the best of the French clubs, the 'Villida,' which for the last six years has never been beaten excepting by the English; and now that they have imitated the English style of rowing to a certain extent, have become formidable opponents, especially since they practise every day, winter as well as summer.

Although the English club counts twenty members, they still want a few good oars among them, and they hope that next season will bring them a few, though they are so much elated with this year's success, that if an English crew were to offer to race them, it is more than probable that they would accept the challenge.

The Captain and Professor made their first cruise in the 'Undine' on the day that we arrived at Asnières, and a tolerably stiff ten miles pull it was, too, against wind and stream, and amidst pouring rain. The Doctor steered the four-oar, and certainly we have seen many a worse crew on the Cam than that which manned the 'Eva' that afternoon.

We left the boats at St. Cloud that night, intending to return the next day; for the Emperor had offered some prizes of Sèvres porcelain to be raced for, and some good pulling (that is, for the Seine) might be expected.

On our return to Paris we called on a very kind-hearted friend, who said he thought we should run a great risk in travelling in such an unprotected manner along the unfrequented parts of France.

'The bargees are a ruffianly set of fellows,' said he, 'and would make an end of three such little fellows as you in a very short time, were it only for the sake of a few francs; so whatever you do, I'd recommend you not to show more money than there is any necessity for. I don't mind young fellows having plenty of rope. I'm not one of those who would keep them in-doors all their young days; but I do think this expedition of yours is rather foolhardy.' But we had calculated the cost of our work before we began, and although one of the crew, after the above hints, suggested the propriety of taking a brace of pistols with us in case of accident, he was over-ruled, and we went defenceless, at least as regarded any artificial weapons.

It was a lovely morning when we arrived at St. Cloud by rail from Paris, but we learnt, to our great disappointment, that the 'Maire' of St. Cloud had put off the regatta, because the day before was wet—a curious reason, we thought, for postponing a boat-race.

However, it was a gay scene enough; the fountains of St. Cloud were playing, and a great number of people had collected on the banks to witness the regatta. All their racing boats were there also, from the odd French boat, which by the regulation measures in breadth one half her length, down to the out-rigger four-oar and the single-streak *funny* of the English club, not forgetting our own little pair-oar.

The costume of the French crews is something wonderful: one has an entire suit of black, another a suit of two colours arranged in a very quaint manner, one half of the jersey and one arm being red, and the other half blue, perhaps, and the opposite quarters of the body coloured in a similar manner. One club adopts the harlequin costume. The immense flags they carry are large enough to sink a boat of an ordinary size.

An ineffectual attempt having been made to get up a race between the four-oars, the stroke of the 'Eva' pluckily offered to race, in the funny, the best French crew, and having started, manfully kept his distance, some little way a-head of them, during two-thirds of the race, but the funny being built for a lighter weight, and he not being at all accustomed to sculling, was obliged to give in, and pull gently towards shore.

The Captain of the 'Undine' now tried the funny, and finding it much better suited to his weight, declared that he would not at all mind racing the

A BOATING DINNER. 17

French four-oar; but they were already too much exhausted with the stiff pull that Stroke had given them; therefore as no one was inclined to get up another race, we all made off again for Asnières, having sent the 'Undine' on through Paris, to a boat-house near the Pont de Marie, to be kept there till we should call for her on the following day.

Mr. Arthur had kindly invited us to join his crew in a boating dinner, which was to be given at his country residence—Bougeval. Thither, therefore, we repaired, as soon as we had stowed the boat away at Asnières. The dinner, an excellent one, and the songs and toasts that followed (intrinsically English, the whole of them), would have cheered the heart of any 'true Briton,' for an Englishman can rarely do much work unless he begins with a dinner, or at least has it in prospect.

The sight of a number of young fellows sitting uneasily, even upon soft cushions—the complaints of blisters—the talk about Bow's continual shirking —of the nuisance that Three is to Bow (at least so the latter declares), for he is always 'chucking water'—of all the mysteries concerning rowlocks and toe-straps—of stretchers and bottom-boards— of out-riggers and spirts—tended in no small degree

C

to carry back the Captain and Professor to the old scenes and old times—

> When not unlike a galley-slave they tugged an honoured oar,
> Which decked their heads with laurels and their hands with many a sore,
> Much rather rowed a Cambridge *Eight* than read of Greek Trireme
> And far preferred the muddy Cam to Tiber's yellow stream.

In the course of the evening the crew of the 'Villida' joined us; a very pleasant set of men, rather too excitable for steady work, but, like the members of the English club, they seem embued with a spirit of generous emulation, though, if the truth were known, the latter looked down upon them rather. Some of the French crews have refused to race with the English, because their boat is so much lighter and narrower. On hearing this the English ordered a boat to be built of the same dimensions as the French boat—viz., in width just half her length. We saw this craft when she was nearly finished, but no pulling man would ever have imagined that she was intended for a boat. However, it shows much spirit to have such a thing built, and we have since heard, that even in this they have again succeeded in thrashing their opponents.

THE START.

In the out-rigger four-oar they have beaten fourteen French boats at one time, although during the race one of the crew broke his rowlock, and they were therefore reduced to two oars only, and beyond this had, of course, two dead weights in the boat.

But we must hasten our departure from Paris, for the Professor can only be absent from England during six weeks, and we have a plenty of work cut out for that time. We begged our friend Arthur, if he felt disposed, to join us at Strasburg, which he promised to do if he possibly could. He wished us every success in our undertaking, and we, wishing him heartily farewell, hoisted our union-jack for the first time, and at length had fairly started on a voyage, destined to extend over nearly 1000 miles of country.

When we had passed the junction of the Marne with the Seine, some little way out of Paris, we moored our craft to the bank, and, jumping ashore, commenced our meal of stewed beef and carrots, rejoicing in the first use of *the* dish, *the* bottle, and *the* glass, which the considerate Professor had provided as part of the cargo of the boat, and we all declared we had never before enjoyed a meal so much as this.

Towards nightfall we were somewhat surprised at the terrible quacking and cackling that proceeded from the neighbouring meadows, and fancied at first that it must have proceeded from a large flock of geese or ducks, but the Professor informed us that the noise (which was sometimes so loud that we had to speak in a tolerably high tone of voice to be heard) was the nightly chorus of numberless frogs—a more musical race in their own idea than the English ones, no doubt. We, however, should not have been at all sorry to have dispensed with their harmonious cra - - ack, cra - - ack, were we able to have done so. Our first real halt on the banks of the Seine was not a very propitious one. The auberge at which we had pulled up (a lone house—for we could get no lodgings in the village of Juvisy) was full of bargees, who, half drunk, were quarrelling to their hearts' content, making, as may be supposed, even more noise than the frogs outside. The landlady also at first refused to have anything to do with us, the Professor having paid her his first visit in boating costume, but eventually admitted us to a sleeping apartment, the beds in which were so damp that the Professor lay down on the tile floor, declaring all the time that he wished he had slept in the boat, and the Captain and Doctor, as they had done once before this summer in Devonshire, spread their mackintoshes over the damp bed, and slept soundly.

The banks of the Seine above Paris, though not so fine as at least one side of the river below, towards Rouen, are still very pretty; the villages are numerous and straggling, with a large country house here and there (or *châteaux*, as they should be called; for every country house, however small, so long as it possesses a turret of some sort, is named a *château*). The land near the river is generally fertile, and well wooded. We had a strong stream to contend with in some places, for the water was much higher than usual; and although we bathed frequently, we felt the heat a good deal, the more so, perhaps, as we had not yet got into regular swing for work.

Passing Corbeil we soon made Melun, the ancient Melodunum, and now the chief town of the department of 'Seine et Marne.' Here the stream was so strong, being confined in a narrow channel, that we had hard work to pull through the bridge, and the sight of our difficulties caused a good deal of merriment to the inhabitants, many of whom had assembled on the bridge, having espied us at a little distance from the town.

Another day's pull brought us to Montereau. Here we rested, for from the neighbouring hills a fine view may be obtained of the surrounding country, the winding of the Seine below, and the junction of the Yonne with the Seine just above the town. It was on these heights of Surville that Napoleon, on the evening of the 17th of February, 1814, assembled the French troops in imposing masses, commanding the bridge and the town beneath them. The Artillery of the Guard was placed on either side of the road, near the cross, and the Emperor took his station in person amidst the guns, to direct their fire, for the enemy still held the town. Such was his eagerness to annihilate the dense masses of the enemy crowding over the bridge, that he himself, resuming his old occupation of gunner, with his own hand, as at Toulon, levelled and pointed a cannon upon them. —*Alison.*

Pictures of Napoleon in this attitude abound in the smallest villages through which we passed; but it would be difficult to say which is the greater favourite, this or another picture representing the Emperor on horseback at Waterloo, with the forelegs of his charger stuck out in a most wonderful manner.

Our landlady evinced a great thirst for the English language, and, we believe, had got as far as the word *yes* before we left Montereau. When she learnt that one of us knew but little of the French language, she exclaimed, 'Ah, pauvre homme!' with such an evident air of commiseration, that it was impossible to laugh, she spoke with so much simplicity and earnestness. But we must not find fault with her; she took great care of us, and studied our comfort, during the short stay we made, with as much attention as if we had belonged to her own family.

CHAPTER IV.

DIJON—LE CÔTE D'OR.

We were a gallant company,
Riding o'er land, and sailing o'er sea,
We forded the river, and clomb the high hill,
  * * * *
Whether we lay in the cave or the shed,
Our sleep fell soft on the hardest bed;
Whether we couch'd in our rough capote,
Or the rougher plank of our gliding boat,
Or stretch'd on the beach *with the canvas* spread
As a pillow beneath the resting head,
Fresh we woke upon the morrow.
The Siege of Corinth.

THE current in the Yonne is much swifter than that in the Seine, the bottom more rocky, and the bends of the river more sudden; in one part it was so shallow, that not knowing the channel, we had to jump out and march with the boat up stream. We had not, however, proceeded far in this manner, when we learnt, from the sudden disappearance of the Professor, that the stream was again navigable. About thirty miles from Montereau is Sens, a pretty little town, or rather city, of about 10,000 inhabitants. The cathedral is already world-known, and the Treasury contains the complete pontifical dress of St. Thomas of Canterbury, who came here from England in the year 1164.

'The walls of Sens,' says Murray, 'exhibit in the lower portion, magnificent remains of Roman, some say of Gaulish, masonry:' we took it for granted, for we did not see them.

After passing Joigny, a quaint old town scarcely accessible owing to the steepness of its numerous streets, the river leads us to Laroche, the commencement of the Canal de Bourgogne. On our way, the Professor dropped his fishing rod overboard, and as it was rather too good to lose, the Captain jumped in after it; and after a vigorous chace of about six minutes, during which time he disappeared once or twice, succeeded in capturing the runaway.

On entering any of the canals in France, it is

necessary to apply to the Bureau of the Director, to obtain a *laissez-passer*, that is, a document (for which a small sum is demanded, according to the length of the canal) to serve as a passport through the canal, and to be endorsed by the *éclusier* or sluice-keeper at each lock.

Our work here was very different to that against stream—more satisfactory, for we got over double the distance in the same time, but apt to make us lazy, since there was so little work to be done. Our course was more monotonous, as far as concerns the scenery in our immediate neighbourhood: the canal often runs for miles without a bend or turn of any kind; then we have high stiff banks with a road or pathway on the top, and on the outside of this, as one might almost say, a *wall* of poplar trees, which, by the bye, were very acceptable sometimes, for they served as a good protection from the sun, the heat of which was beginning to tell upon our hands, faces, and feet especially.

At the junction of two small streams, the Armance and Armançon (along the valley of which last the canal takes its course, and by which it is fed), stands St. Florentin, a pretty little town with a church, which, though sadly neglected, is still a fair example of Second Pointed Gothic. The

Messieurs are Inspectors of the Canal?

London: John W. Parker & Son, West Strand, 1854.

CANAL INSPECTORS. 27

Abbey of Pontigny, about fifteen miles distant (once the residence of St. Thomas à Becket, and also of Stephen Langton, Archbishop of Canterbury, whose tomb is still to be found in Chichester Cathedral), contains the shrine of the English St. Edmund. But though the Captain especially wished to visit the abbey, we had no time for an excursion so far out of our route.

Many of the sluice-keepers fancy that we are inspectors of the canal, a position which we, of course, endeavour to keep up with all becoming dignity. We look very important—take notes as to the state of some of the locks, and at others gravely examine the account books submitted to our inspection. This, of course, insures to us an amount of civility and attention that, perhaps, we should not otherwise meet with.

In towing barges, &c., along the canal, horses are seldom, if ever, used. The method generally adopted is this: when (as is frequently the case) they are one family travelling with the barge, the mother on one side of the canal and the son on the other, with a rope each, haul the barge along, necessarily at a very slow pace (say a mile and a half in the hour), while the father stays on board, smokes his pipe, and steers the barge.

The surrounding country gets much more interesting as we proceed, till we come in sight of the church of St. Pierre, which overlooks the dull old town Tonnerre, and here we are in the midst of hills, small, but often steep and picturesquely rugged.

We here learnt that the Emperor was to pass along this canal in a few days, and the good people supposed that we were the engineers appointed to conduct his small steamer for him. Some opined that ours was the boat in which he was to travel; while others said it was only the convoy.

Often, during the middle of the day, we would stop near a lock, and spreading the canvas of the boat to do the work of a table cloth, lie at full length under the shade of the poplars, dispatch our luncheon, then try our luck with the rod and line. Sometimes we had very good sport, for the canal abounds in tench and pike, not to mention smaller fry. It was on one of these occasions that the lock-keeper declared that he could not imagine what it was coming down the canal. He had seen us land some little way off, and had in his simplicity supposed that we were ladies bathing.

It is still problematical for what reason the district we were now entering is called the *Côte d'Or;*

LE CÔTE D'OR.

whether it derives its name from the range of hills, which are of a deep copper hue, or the great wealth arising from the abundant produce of the vines in this department. The vineyards along which we passed, and even as far as we could see on either side of us, were very rich, though it is said that all the ground about here is not equally productive; but there can be no doubt that it is the finest country of vines in Europe.

On arriving at Montbard we saw the chateau in which Buffon, the naturalist, was born. The revolutionists have made sad havoc here, and the tower which formed his study, standing in one corner of the extensive gardens, is now a mere ruin, nothing but the bare walls remaining, and these fast going to decay.

At length we reached Dijon, and a long way off the distant blue outline of the Jura mountains just makes its appearance above the horizon. In our peregrination of Dijon, we came upon no less than three desecrated churches, one being used as a vegetable market, another as a corn exchange, and a third as a stable for the cavalry! We called on Mr. Baumgarten, the engineer of the Canal du Rhôn au Rhin, to gain some information from him concerning the practicability of our route, and to inquire where we could find a large map of the canal, for we had tried in vain at Dijon. He met us in his hall, and informed us that if it was our intention to travel by water from Dijon to the Rhine, we had nothing to do but to go! We thanked him for his kindness and wished him good morning.

As we were on our way to the Palace (Palais des Etats; and formerly belonging to the Dukes of Burgundy), the Doctor suddenly cried out—

'Hallo, Captain! there's a charming filly, by George!'

'Charming filly! where?' said the Captain.

'Just on a-head, there, a little way—don't you see? Dark chesnut mane, rather goodish eye, clean about the pastern; *leetle* too high in the wither for me—but there's action for you! I wonder if she'd be quiet to drive in double harness? inclined at all to bolt with a fellow, eh, Cap'n?'

'My dear fellow,' replied the Captain, 'what are you raving about? I don't see anything in the shape of a horse in the—'

'Horse, you muff! come along, I say, there she goes into the bookseller's, and I want a conversation book.'

'Stop a bit,' said the Professor, 'you don't

DIJON. 31

want a conversation book, you know, they are not much use to anybody; besides, I don't intend to give you any money to buy one, I can tell you.'

And so the poor man was constrained to go and pretend to be very much interested in some prints in the bookseller's window. He was doomed to be disappointed, however, for his *filly* had bolted.

Dijon itself is situated in a large plain (some parts of which are frequently overflown by the waters of the Saône), bounded by the range of the Côte d'Or on one side, and the Jura on the other. The public buildings of Dijon are remarkable for their very massive character, the churches have almost ' a fortress-like appearance in solidity.' The *flèche* of St. Benigne (the cathedral, which is somewhat celebrated) is 'an elongated pyramid or obelisk of wood, and possesses no beauty except from its height and its general harmony with the rest of the structure.' It is, however, also remarkable from the fact that the angles of the spire do not run in straight lines from the base to the top, but are twisted spirally round the flèche; this adds greatly to the beauty of the building, although whether it was built thus in the first instance is a matter of doubt.

In the Museum the things most worthy of note

are the tombs of Philippe-le-Hardi and his son Jean-sans-Peur; being very similar in construction, it will suffice to mention the particulars of one only. 'The sides of the tomb,' that is of the father's, 'are ornamented with singular beauty; instead of niches or panels filled with statues in basso-relievo, the dado is here surrounded by a miniature cloister, worked most delicately and elaborately in the finest alabaster. The little pillars, which stand quite free, sustain canopies and finials of the richest pattern, and in each division are the statues of one or two friars. All are represented as mourners, but with the most skilful variety of feeling : one in all the anguish of grief, a second equally afflicted but tranquilly resigned, a third stupified with sorrow; all as true as if you had the convent before you. The draperies are admirable, and whether we consider the goodness of the drawing or the skill of the execution, we must confess that it would be hardly possible to rival the skill of Claus Slater, the Dutchman (for he was the artist), in the present day.'—*Murray.*

CHAPTER V.

ST. JEAN DE L'OSNE.

Quoique leurs chapeaux soient bien laids ;
Moi j'aime les Anglais :
Ils ont un si bon caractère !
Comme ils sont polis, et surtout
Que leurs plaisirs sont de bon goût.

Béranger.

NE evening we were gradually nearing St. Jean de l'Osne, a small town, which, from the primitive customs of its inhabitants, would seem to be cut off from the rest of the world. We had just left the Canal de Bourgogne, and had entered the Saône, whose course we had to follow for some few miles previous to our reaching the Canal du Rhône au Rhin. The

Professor left us for a moment to get the necessary papers, *laissez-passer*, &c., and in the mean time the collection of small boys, who had discovered us at some distance from the town, continued adding to their numbers until they assumed the appearance of a respectable crowd.

Having procured the *laissez-passer*, which cost us the extravagant sum of one penny, we pulled on towards the town, accompanied by the crowd of people on the bank, most of whom were breathless from another cause than that of astonishment, long before they reached the bridge of St. Jean de l'Osne. The Professor again landed, and found a very comfortable lodging at the Hôtel de Commerce, not very far from the spot at which we had set him ashore, with a convenient court-yard in front, where we could safely stow the boat; accordingly we commenced unloading her, and carried the knapsacks, &c., into the hotel.

Meanwhile the crowd was still increasing, and the excitement becoming intense; everybody was rushing about here and there, to catch if it were a glimpse only of *les Anglais* and their *petite chaloupe*. Having cleared the boat of her light cargo, we ran her ashore and commenced carrying

Arrival at St Jean de Lune.

London: John W. Parker & Son, West Strand, 1854.

ST. JEAN DE L'OSNE. 35

her towards the yard. Astonishment was depicted in every face; there was a momentary silence throughout the whole crowd—then a murmur of applause —a general shout, and away the ' Undine' swam as it were upon the heads of the crowd. She was carried off, and there would have been no stopping her had not one of us, running under her whole length, managed to seize her by the bow, and so guide her into the yard, otherwise there is no knowing what might have become of her by this time.

When once in the court, and safely laid on her keel, the *jabber* began, for as many as could had accompanied her into the yard, and almost distracted us with the number and variety of their questions. The noise they made was deafening. One would come, and, having his question answered, retire again, and commence a magniloquent discourse to those near him, taking our answer for his subject. The imagination of the natives of St. Jean de l'Osne is extremely fertile, one word being enough for them to make a tale or even write a history. The Professor was informing some ladies that we had crossed the Channel in a steamer; an imaginative bystander instantly caught the word *vapeur*, and away he hastened

D 2

to inform his friends that the three Englishmen had crossed the Channel in their little boat, having exceeded in speed the fastest *vapeur*. The worthy Professor also mentioned that on our way we had stopped at St. Cloud, and that the Emperor had offered prizes to be pulled for there, &c. This was transformed into a rumour that the Emperor, hearing of our adventurous expedition, had himself presented us with a handsome gift at St. Cloud, and that in addition to this we had won no end of cups and gold medals on our way. All these and many other similar rumours, were confirmed by the Doctor's everlasting *oui* to all their inquiries. Had the question been, 'Do you not always make your boat leap over the bridges you meet with *en route?*' the gullible inquirer would have been met with the same invariable *oui, oui*, strengthened, perhaps, by affirmative nods.

But we had pulled all the way from Dijon, and wanting our dinner, were anxious to get rid of our admiring friends as speedily as possible; so, rightly thinking that they would stop to look at us as long as we stayed with the boat, we left them and went in to dinner. Our good landlady supplied us with a capital repast and an excellent bottle of Burgundy, and while we were consuming these she was vainly endeavouring to clear the court. The Gendarmes shortly made their appearance, and were equally surprised with our passports as with ourselves, for being drawn up in English they could not possibly make anything of them, but wisely supposing them all right let them pass.

After dinner we sallied out to see as much of the town as we could by the aid of starlight and gas light, when we were again assailed with multitudinous questions about the boat. The Captain's stock of French was put to the uttermost, while the Doctor continued to converse solely by the aid of pantomimic gesture.

We entered the Café National, and here we were treated with marked respect and civility; every person had something to say to us, everybody something to ask about the expedition or its object. As we came into the room one was heard to exclaim, 'Ah! voilà les trois Anglais venus de Londres dans une petite chaloupe. Tout de même ces Anglais sont une nation très brave et très entreprenante!' The proprietor was very proud of our having patronized his café, and when it was the usual time of closing, insisted on taking us to a large Salle de Danse, situated in the centre of a small park belonging to the town. Here the sensation was, if possible, greater than ever, for having taken our evening walk in the usual costume of straw hat, blue jerseys and flannels, we appeared rather conspicuous; but the curiosity of the people was easily smoothed down on these points, for one more clever and more learned than the rest undertook to inform his companions that *that* was the ordinary style of dress of an English gentleman. The Professor could not refrain from joining in 'the dance,' while he left 'the merry laughing' part of the business to us, for it must be said he cut a very comical figure among the sombre dresses of the natives.

We were in imminent peril here, however, for numbers insisted on our drinking beer with them; and it is probable that had it not been for the well-timed interference of mine host of the café, we should have been torn in pieces through their kindness, though eventually we got off safely, and retired for the night.

At three o'clock the next morning the people began again to collect in the yard, and continued increasing in numbers till nine, for it had been given out the previous night that it was our intention to start at that time in the morning. It was most amusing to hear these people talking about us, each being thoroughly confident that he knew more than his neighbour.

'Mais oui! c'est un veritable bateau à vapeur! Je l'ai entendu dire hier soir par un de ces Anglais. Ils sont huit d'equipage.'

'Non, non! c'est ridicule ce que vous dites là; ils ne sont que six; quatre rames, le gouvernail, et un crampon, voilà ce que fait marcher le bateau! Et tenez! remarquez les places pour les quatre rames," pointing out the rowlocks, which were adapted for double sculling. After our breakfast we were called upon to settle a dispute concerning the uses of the rudder. One man was willing to give up his idea, and own that it really was the *gouvernail* if any of his comrades would inform him to what possible use those strings could be put, but this he defied them to do.

The Captain and Professor, to indulge the people with a true and real notion of the speed we could get on the boat, pulled about a little in front of the town, and the dashing manner in which the bridge was shot earned us an undeserved cheer from the banks, for there was not really the slightest necessity for shipping our oars, yet it was a manœuvre, and much delighted the spectators.

It did not take us long to put our small amount

of baggage into the boat, and we left the scene of our great popularity amidst tumultuous cheering and great waving of handkerchiefs. Pulling merrily away for some distance up the Saône, we overtook a gang of barges to which we fastened our small craft—jumped on board—fraternized with the bargees, and partook of the very tolerable cheer that our companions civilly offered us.

They were much struck with the simple manner in which we lighted our pipes by means of a burning-glass, and every one of them immediately pulled out his pipe and filled it, that he might have it lighted by this *machine diabolique* as they called it. We joined them in some of their French songs as well as we were able, and thus continued during the heat of the day, till arriving at St. Semphorien, we ended our short course on the Saône and took to canal again.

CHAPTER VI.

BESANÇON—LE PETIT QUART D'HEURE.

Oppidum maximum Sequanorum, naturâ loci sic muniebatur ut magnam ad ducendum bellum daret facultatem; propterea quod flumen Dubis, ut circino circumductum pene totum oppidum cingit, reliquum spatium, non est amplius pedum DC., quâ flumen intermittit, mons continet magnâ altitudine, ita ut radices montis ejus ex utrâque parte ripæ fluminis contingunt.—*Cæs. Com.* lib. 1.

AS there were many barges waiting to pass through the double locks which lead from the Saône into the Canal du Rhône au Rhin, we lifted the boat over the bank, to the surprise of a number of bargees, who presently drew around us, and paid us (as we presumed from their volubility of speech, and the emphasis they laid on many high-sounding words,) no end of compliments.

This canal is not kept in such good order as those in Burgundy; many of the locks, to our annoyance, worked very heavily; we therefore, in our capacity of canal inspectors, were constrained to take more copious notes, and frequently to complain of the sad state the account books were in.

The fall of water in some of these locks is very great, being sometimes as much as fifteen or sixteen feet, though generally averaging from ten to twelve; the water comes rushing in through the sluice, when opened, with great force, and forms, in fact, a complete *jet d'eau* of about two feet six inches square. It need not be hinted how very necessary it is to keep the boat out of the reach of this spout, or to prevent her scraping against the sides of the lock; but this is not always such an easy matter, there being so great a commotion of water in the lock. We calculated that it took us six minutes to pass a lock when one of the crew assisted the *éclusier*, and about twenty when we all remained in the boat.

Arriving at Dôle, a small but very picturesque looking town, with an extremely interesting church

AN AUSTRIAN BARGEE.

and remains of extensive fortifications, we were inclined to stop for the night, especially when we learnt that from the heights of the Jura near the town, the snowy top of Mont Blanc may be seen, being one hundred miles distant as the crow flies; but having still a long evening before us, we preferred pulling on again till we reached Rochefort. This village, situated on the right bank of the River Doubs, is flanked by a perpendicular cliff of sandrock, from the top of which a fine view of this splendid river is to be obtained.

While we were enjoying our supper, an Austrian bargee who was sitting with his friends in the same room as ourselves, became very merry, and indulged himself and us with the *jodel*.

'Ah!' said the Professor, 'c'est le Ranz des Vaches, n'est-ce pas?'

'Non,' replied the Austrian; for he did not seem to like being interfered with, and not having perhaps the clearest notion of what he was about (which he sufficiently proved afterwards), abused our worthy Professor like a pickpocket.

The Doctor got a little apprehensive, not much liking the idea of stopping in the same house, much less in the same room for the night with 'the sanguinary bargee.' The Professor, however, being a man of peace, quietly let the matter drop for a little time, then migrated to the bargee's table and, not too pointedly, offered him a little wine, which he immediately accepted, and wished us success. The ice being thus broken, we soon became more intimate, and eventually won the bargee's heart, by talking with him a few words of German. The former unpleasantness was forgotten, and he politely offered again to amuse us with his peculiar *jodel;* he got very excited—flung his cap, arms and legs about in a very ludicrous manner; but at last was so obliging as to invite the Captain to share his bed with him for the night, which proffered honour, however, the Captain was fain to decline, for many reasons.

The Doctor was obliged to overcome his prejudices, and sleep in the same room with ourselves and three bargees, of whom our Austrian friend was one. It need hardly be said that we slept soundly, and awoke in the morning with an appetite not at all lessened when we learnt that there was nothing to be had for breakfast. The bargees made theirs of a glass of gin and a pipe of tobacco, but this diet being hardly in consonance with our perhaps bigoted notions, we made off to a neighbouring millowner, and having related to him our

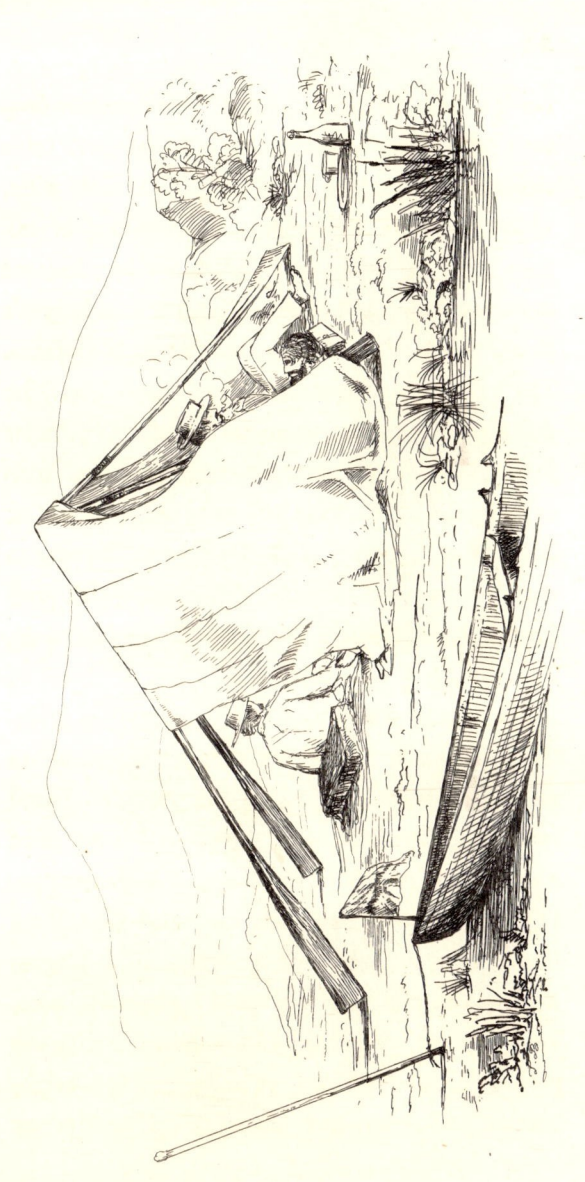

On the banks of the Douls.

London: John W. Parker & Son. West Strand. 1854.

piteous condition, he presented us with a bowl of milk enough for six. We were afterwards joined by his son, a respectable young fellow, who accompanied us in the boat two or three miles up the river, and he sang some French songs, while we pulled lazily along.

But before we started we were glad to have a bathe again in something like clear fresh water, for, with exception the Saône, we had been obliged to bathe in the canals ever since we left the Yonne. The water of the Doubs is beautifully clear —much colder, and therefore much more refreshing than that in the canals; and another advantage, over and above the changed scenery, was the improvement in the fishing, which added not a little to the enjoyment of a pleasant hour after a day's work.

This, our first day on the Doubs, was one of the most beautiful for river scenery that we had yet enjoyed. But the sun being very powerful, we made a tent of the oars, sculls, and canvas covering of the boat, under which we rested three hours, taking an alternate snooze and a sketch of the neighbouring hills, for we were now in the midst of the Jura.

As we ascended the river, the banks on either side became more and more rocky, until at length we entered a defile, which continues for several miles, and along the bottom of which the Doubs takes its course, having forced itself through these hills on its way towards the Saône.

Between St. Vic and Aveney there is a tunnel to admit a short canal, pierced through one of the hills, around the foot of which the river flows; it is only about 600 yards long, but by its aid one saves about four miles of the river, which is very shallow just here.

Twilight was falling in when we passed the tunnel, and we had to make away with all possible speed for an auberge, which we heard was about five miles off. We were quite benighted before we arrived there; and consequently missed the view of some very fine hills, which rose immediately from the right bank of the river, and as it seemed, here and there a ruin overhanging the stream. It was so very dark for the last few miles that we were compelled to send our Coxswain forward to steer. About half-past ten we reached the auberge, which we found was no great distance from Aveney, and of course greatly astonished the very masculine-looking landlady, who assisted us in clearing the boat. This was certainly the roughest place we

CLOSE QUARTERS.

had hitherto encountered. After our supper we entered *the* bed room, for it seemed to do service for the whole of the house, and is worth describing. A large room, that is, large for a road-side inn, being about thirty feet by twenty, is divided lengthways into three equal spaces, the two adjacent to the wall being appropriated for the beds, which are stretched one above another, in the same fashion as berths on board a passenger vessel; the walls and ceiling of the room seem to have been battened with reeds, and then daubed over with mud, which they told us kept them very warm in winter; we can testify to its warmth in summer, but then there were nine other people sleeping in the room. However, we rested as soundly as if on the softest bed of down, nor were we prevented from dropping off to sleep by the deep sonorous breathing, that issued from under the coverlids of our companions.

We descended from our dormitory in the morning, by the same ladder we had used the night before, and after a bathe and a breakfast, started for Besançon, hoping to reach the city before the heat of the day.

We were continually being told such different

stories, however, about the distance from one place to another, that it was quite impossible to say when we started in the morning where we should get by nightfall. We had proceeded some three hours when we demanded of a native how far we were from Besançon. He replied, 'Un petit quart d'heure.' We then pulled on for half-an-hour, and asked again the same question and met with the same reply, and after another half hour's work we sighted Besançon, but we were then full twenty minutes before we reached the town. Admiring as we approached them the strongly fortified citadel and the abrupt heights which surround both it and the town, we followed the course of the river, making almost a complete circuit of the town, which may be said to stand on a peninsula. Julius Cæsar, in his *Commentaries* on this part of the world, says that the isthmus which prevents the town from being wholly insulated, is only 500 feet across; but either his feet must have been above the ordinary size, or else perhaps he was not so precise in his admeasurement as we were.

While the Doctor and Professor mounted the hill to inspect the fortifications and its commanding position (for further particulars concerning the latter vide the above-mentioned *Commentaries* and Murray's *Handbook*), the Captain invested capital in a brown holland coat, which was better adapted for carrying mud than either his alpaca or bright blue jersey. He had been so extravagant in the matter of the coat (cost five francs) that we were compelled afterwards to leave the Doctor in pawn while we went to seek a fresh supply of funds to pay for some ices we had indulged in. And rather tired he was of his position by the time we called for him, for we had in the interim gone to visit the 'Chamars,' which is said to occupy the site as well as retain in part the name of the Roman Campus Martius.

'Papa!' said a little girl, as we walked along under the citadel in the cool of the evening; 'Papa, what are those three gentlemen in lemon-coloured pantaloons?'

'They are three officers, my little one, who have had the management of the works in the construction of several railways, and now they are going to make one from Dijon to Mulhouse,' &c.

We had every reason to believe that this conversation was prolonged for some time, for though we could not distinguish anything further that was

E

said concerning us, we saw them and their friends eyeing us minutely for the next half hour.

The following morning, as we were engaged in sponging out the boat, one of the crew who was 'holding on' let her drift with the stream to the full length of the painter, when she stopped, of course, with a jerk which very nearly sent the Captain spinning out into the water.

Cap. Now then!—'vast there, I say; just haul taut and belay, will you!

Prof. No occasion for German just yet, Cap'n; keep it till we get to Germany.*

At eleven A.M. we left Besançon, passing along through beautiful scenery which Murray says resembles the Meuse between Liege and Namur— really, it is much finer.

---

* The Professor's acquaintance with the sea has been derived exclusively from crossing the Channel in steamers.

CHAPTER VII.

CHANGE FOR A NAPOLEON.

Master Humphreys. The comely maid! Such term
   not half the sum
Of her rich beauty gives! Were rule to go
By loveliness, I know not in the court
Or city, lady might not fitly serve
That lady serving maid.—*The Love Chase.*

River Doubs is *canalized*, if one may coin a word; that is, it is rendered navigable, by numerous weirs, and at the side of each is a set of locks by means of which barges, boats, or rafts of timber, may be raised or lowered as required.

It was at one of these that the boat had a narrow

escape. The Professor had lost his hat in the water, and we, in our anxiety to regain it, were not conscious of our approach to the weir; fortunately, the Captain, who was steering, discovered our position, though only in time to spring to the bank and hold on by one of the rudder strings while the boat swung round with her bow half over the top of the waterfall. It was hard work even then to prevent her from being carried down stream, for there was a great body of water rushing over the weir.

About this time our small stock of linen running rather short, the Captain undertook the office of *blanchisseuse;* the jerseys, &c., were washed in very little time—and dried in still less, for it was so intensely hot, that the very hills seemed as if they could not breathe; in fact, we preferred bathing *in* our clothes to-day, that they might keep us cool by evaporation afterwards.

Attempts were made to teach the Doctor to swim, but they proved utterly futile; he positively will not float.

The banks of the river about these parts are very fine, being quite equal and very similar to the Neckar above Heidelberg, though on a larger scale. Where they do not rise immediately from the water's edge in rocky precipices, the adjacent hills, covered with vines, slope down towards the river, being met at the bottom by productive meadows, studded with farmhouses, the white fronts and quaint roofs of which add not a little to the cheerfulness of the scene. The tow-path also, along the banks, is kept in such beautiful order that you might almost fancy yourself in private grounds.

Towards evening we approached Baume, a tolerable village near the river, and famous for its pâtés and fish, which last we can answer for as deserving notice, for we had capital sport, baiting the hook with a grasshopper at least double the size of those in England. We stopped short of Baume, however, and were conducted by a very civil and complimentary old Abbé to an auberge, one of the most curious we had hitherto come across. We were compelled to take our supper in a double-bedded room which was already occupied, but afterwards were fain to retire to the kitchen to smoke our pipes. The Captain and Doctor slept on the staircase, and the Professor in a four-bedded room which was well filled with men and children.

In the morning, on going to the boat, we found that our old friend the Abbé had informed the inhabitants of Baume of our arrival, for many of them had come down to see these wonderful men and their curious *barquette*.* They seemed somewhat amused as well as surprised at our primitive mode of performing the ablutionary part of our toilette; for we invariably left our rooms, or wherever we had slept, towel in hand, and made for the nearest and most convenient spot for a plunge into the river. This was the more necessary, as frequently there was no apparatus provided for washing; or if on our stopping at any place of more than ordinary pretension there *was* a towel and a basin in our room, we could rarely find more water than would have left us a wine glass full each. On this point the Professor, who knows a good deal of the manners and customs of the inhabitants of the interior of France, informed us that the usual mode of washing among the peasants is this:

On Sundays, or on an average once a week, they will fill their mouths with cold water, and keeping it there for some time (to avoid, as he supposes, any unnecessary waste of fuel in warming the water), throw the head back and allow the water to trickle

---

* Our craft was designated by numerous different names, such as bateau, barque, canot, batelotte, chaloupe, nacelle, &c.; and afterwards in Germany, as Boot, Bootchen, Schiff, Schifflein, &c.

'HOTEL CHARGES.'

over the face, which is then rubbed with the bare hand till the fluid has evaporated. The process of combing the hair he supposes to take place about once a month. Now it was generally a rule of ours to conform to the customs of the country we were passing through, but this fashion being somewhat beyond us, we resorted to the method above-mentioned of taking an early dip.

This day we still continued to find the same sort of bold scenery along the banks, which is frequently and agreeably relieved by the sight of numerous and elegant suspension bridges that span the river. So slight are the suspension chains, that one wonders how they can sustain the weight of the bridge, much less anything passing over it. Five miles from Baume a mass of naked rock five hundred feet high, of the most picturesque form, overhangs the road, which has barely room to pass between it and the river.

The charge at our halting-place to-day would supply ample *materiel* for some of the recent correspondents of the *Times* on hotel charges. We had a dinner of five courses, beginning with soup and ending with salad, two bottles of wine, one of beer, curaçoa after dinner, beds, and breakfast for three, and another bottle of wine to take with us, for which the total demand, including attendance, amounted to five francs; that is, not one shilling and fivepence each! We met with several other instances of extraordinary moderation in our hotel bills, but this was the lowest during the whole of our trip.—Took our *siesta* to-day on a small strip of land between the canal and the river, for in many parts we leave the river for three or four miles, thus avoiding the frequent bends of the stream. Just where we stopped there is a canal, at a level of perhaps twenty feet above the river, half of its channel being cut in the hill side, and the other half built up. It formed a very pretty and at the same time to us novel feature in the scene—this terrace of water reminding one somewhat of the course of the railway at Dawlish on the South Devon line, though of course the surrounding scenery is somewhat different. Along the whole of this level the canal is necessarily much narrower; in fact it is only wide enough to allow us to scull through, and the Captain walked on a-head to ascertain if there were a barge or any other craft coming to meet us, for in this case we should have been compelled to lift the boat out of the water; but fortunately we only met one impediment—a raft of timber. Amused ourselves in a chase after a large water-snake that had disturbed us whilst fishing, and after some little dodging about with the boat, managed to kill the reptile. He measured between four and five feet in length, and had but recently made his meal of a large frog, which we discovered whole in the snake's inside whilst we were dispatching him.

The inhabitants of Clerval, the next place of any importance we came too, were equally surprised with those of St. Jean de l'Osne; but rather than stop to receive all their congratulations, having provided ourselves with sufficient food for a luncheon, we left the town. It is a pretty little place, with by far the greater part of it lying on the left bank of the river; a few houses on the other side are built against the rock which forms the base of a line of hills one thousand feet high. We got into difficulties in leaving Clerval, having taken the wrong side of a long island ; and having expended some time and trouble in pulling up a rapid, we were obliged to float down again, though not without peril to the boat, for she grounded several times, and we were more than once obliged to jump out and lift her over some rocks which we had easily avoided in going up stream.

The drive along the banks here must be very

beautiful; for from below Ile-sur-Doubs on to Montbelliard, the high road runs close to the stream the whole way, following the windings of the river, between well-wooded hills which rise on either side to the height of two hundred and fifty or three hundred feet.

Having left the Doubs, which takes a sudden turn near Montbelliard, we came upon a glorious view of the Vosges mountains, which looked all the grander on account of the flatness of the interjacent country. The level of the canal being here somewhat higher than that of the ground on either side of the banks, we had an extensive prospect during a good day and a half's work, terminated by the Vosges on one side and the beginning of the Swiss mountains on the other.

We were now on the highest level above the sea that we should attain throughout our voyage. The canal is here fed by a small river—the Ill, and its waters henceforth flow in different directions, that portion behind us being carried by the Doubs, Saône, and Rhône, into the Mediterranean, and that before us flowing by the Rhine into the German ocean.

At Froidefontaine, a small village we passed with a very appropriate name, there were *fêtes* going on,

A CHACE.

and on our leaving the place, half-a-dozen young ladies of the village proposed running after us. As we did not pull hard at first they thought it easy work enough, but as we quickened our pace they gradually dropped astern one after another, until at last there was only one left. We asked her if she would take a cruise with us after her hard work, but she declined. We were here supposed to be strolling comedians! This we felt rather keenly to be sure, but we hardly knew whether we were most snubbed here or at Courcelles, where the people imagined that we were employed in carrying fish for the administration of the canal.

At Valdieu the Coxswain was deeply smitten (not an uncommon occurrence with him, by the bye) with the smiling face of the landlord's fair daughter. He seemed to be suddenly struck with an intense appreciation of the delightful life of a 'patron bargee,' auberge keeper, and dealer in coals, and evidently had an eye to the Father's prosperous business when he spoke in such glowing terms of the daughter. Poor fellow! he suffered a good deal, and for the next two days he was incessantly mingling with his sighs scraps of the little German Volkslied:—

Kein Feuer, keine Kohle kann brennen so heiss,
Als heimliche Liebe, von der Niemand nicht weiss.

And Augustine, sweet little creature, with her black eyes and hands, seemed to be utterly unconscious of the ravages she was making in the breast of another. How should it be otherwise? she was only a child of thirteen after all!

We took a survey of the country about Valdieu, endeavouring to discover some method of avoiding the frequent locks we have to pass; from this point there are no less than forty in eighteen miles, so rapidly does the canal descend. At several of these we lifted the boat over; but finding that it took us equally as long as our former plan, we gave up this fashion.

Unfortunately, at one of these places, the Doctor, who was assisting the *éclusier*, let the crank which opens the sluice fall into the water; and though the Professor dived several times for it, and the Captain progued about with a long hay-rake, much to the amusement of the *éclusier* and his wife, we did not succeed in finding it. There were therefore three francs to pay for the crank, which the *éclusier* of course declared was a bran new one, and having no silver, the Professor must needs make an excursion into the neighbouring village to find change for a Napoleon.

At the principal auberge gold coin is unknown; but reference was made to the rich man of the

CHANGE FOR A NAPOLEON. 61

place, who collected all his family round him for the inspection of the strange coin. The old man, with spectacles on nose, looked and talked very wisely, the sons and nephews ominously wagged their heads ; a consultation in a mixture of horrible German and worse French followed, the conclusion being that the Napoleon was *too yellow.* Two more attempts failed; but at last an adventurous and enterprising wine dealer, who ten years before had seen a Louis d'or, made bold to exchange the Napoleon, declaring that 'he did not care, for if it proved a false one, he had no doubt he could pass it on to some one else.'

He was discovered in his sitting room; two friends who were with him having evidently dropped in for a morning chat. There was a bottle of wine on the table and three tumblers, two of which contained crusts of bread which were being steeped in wine, and the third was half full of soap-suds, for the wine merchant was shaving, and had but half completed his work when the Professor made his appearance. He was asked to sit down a few moments while the painful operation was resumed, and a painful one it seemed to be,—a camel-hair pencil frequently dipped into the soap-suds was as frequently applied to the refractory beard, this being speedily followed by repeated scrapes of a so-called razor. However, his serenity returned when the operation was completed. He then examined the coin and—hung fire. A thought had struck him; the coin must be weighed; but he had no scales,—the tobacconist has scales. Thither accordingly they repaired in haste.

The shop contained wise men whose advice was immediately acted upon; the wine merchant placed a franc in one scale, while he requested the Professor to place his Napoleon in the other. The gold coin outweighed its antagonist, and all declared it to be genuine!

Thirty-seven out of the forty locks we passed to-day; though from the constant delays we did not get over as much ground as we could have wished. Stopt for the night at Silicem, a small place, where we found the people dressed somewhat after the Swiss fashion, and speaking a sort of German. Though still in France we found great difficulty in making ourselves understood, and also in understanding the people, the more so, perhaps, from their being disobliging and surly in this part of the world. The Professor was told that his German was like the German that they read in books, and not that which was spoken.

As we approached Silicem, and night was closing

SILICEM.

in, we observed a thick mist rising in the meadows near the canal, and while we were yet some distance from the village, the malaria which issued from the frequent pools of water in the neighbourhood powerfully affected both the Doctor and Captain, causing a feeling of giddiness, similar to the peculiar sensation that the motion of a ship imparts. The Professor wished to stay with the boat all night, as we could find no convenient place to leave her, but he wisely yielded to the advice of the Doctor, who told him that he would run a great and he thought unnecessary risk in so doing, the air being (as we believed) impregnated with unwholesome exhalations.

We have just caught sight of the Schwartzwald, and have determined on taking the Rhine, near Basle, instead of going, as we had intended, to Strasburg by canal.

CHAPTER VIII.

STORMS NEAR BASLE.

> Then did he make heaven's vault to resound
> With rounce, robble, bobble,
> Of ruffe raffe roaring,
> With thwicke thwacke thurly bouncing.
>
> STANYHURST. *Trans. Virg.*

HE principal mass of the Vosges Mountains lies between Giromany and the valley of Breusch; they are about one hundred and twenty miles in extent, running parallel to the Rhine, and separating its basin from that of the Moselle. They consist chiefly of rounded dome-shaped hills, abounding in forests, and often turfed at the top. The bulk or thickest mass of the Vosges rises between the Ballon d'Alsace (4124 feet), the Donon (3314 feet), and the Ballon de Sultz, the highest of all (4693 feet). The rivers Seine, Saône, Moselle, and Saar, rise in the Vosges. The finest view of this extensive range of mountains is to be obtained between Montbelliard and Mulhausen, which last place is a large manufacturing town; in fact, one of the most important in the whole of France. We did not stop long here, for like most manufacturing towns, it has a very dirty and uninviting appearance.

Pulled on to a small island at the junction of the Basle and Strasburg Canal, and proceeded to take our mid-day meal under the shade of some poplar trees, but were vigorously assailed by the clattering tongues and bell-cracked voices of an army of Blanchisseuses on an opposite bank.

> From the shadow which the coppice
> Flings across the rippling stream,
> Did I hear a sound of music—
> Was it thought, or was it dream?
> There, beside a pile of linen,
> Stretched along the daisied sward,
> Stood a young and blooming maiden—
> 'Twas her thrush-like song we heard—

Which induced us to change our position at least two kilometres further on.

After luncheon, the heat of the sun being excessive, the Captain and Professor determined on walking and pulling the boat along by a rope attached to one of the thwarts, while the Doctor, at all times a great observer of personal comforts, made a screen for himself of the canvas covering of the boat and lay down under it, steering the boat at the same time. We had proceeded in this manner some five or six kilometres when we met one of the fast German barges, empty, and drawn by two horses, with which, however, we could discover no driver.

'Walk on over their line, Professor,' said the Captain, 'and I will stop the horses, so that their rope may drop. Steer inside, Doctor!'

Now the Captain has never evinced any great love for that noble quadruped, the horse; his enemies have therefore said that however well he may manage a boat, his courage fails him when he has anything to do with horses; some have gone so far as to say that he is particularly envious of the man who dares to ride at a five-barred gate or a stone fence.

Whichever was the cause then, either his mismanagement, or incapability on the part of the horses to understand English, the result was certainly most unfortunate ; for instead of stopping the horses, he allowed himself to be carried off his legs, and be dragged some distance by them. Meanwhile the Professor had crossed their rope, and the barge was gradually nearing our bank. The Captain having left the horses, immediately saw the danger, and fearing that the poor little ' Undine' might be shut up between the barge and the bank, telescope fashion, rushed up, shouting ' Cut the line ! cut the line !' for it had become entangled in that of the barge. In the confusion of the moment he was not heard, and the helmsman of the barge, who had been watching our proceedings, steered nearer and nearer our bank by a sort of fascination, until his bows almost touched us. The Captain making a flying buttress of himself, between the barge and bank, endeavoured to fend off the barge and allow space enough for the boat to pass ; but the stern of the barge is coming in with a swing—a prolonged scrape—a crash—and the barge has passed, leaving our poor little craft with two of her thwarts projecting through her wounded side.

' Hum !' said the Doctor, after the approved manner of the medical man. The Professor feared that there was an end of our expedition altogether just as we had sighted the Rhine. ' But let's see the

F 2

extent of the damage,' said the Captain, and jumping on board he took out his clasp knife, and cutting away the broken elbows, forced the thwarts back into their places; and then overhauling the boat fore and aft completely, found that the damage was not so great as might have been anticipated.

Then came a consultation as to whether we should take the boat to Strasburg to be repaired, or try what we could do ourselves. We agreed on adopting the latter course, and accordingly made off for Kembs, a village on the banks of the canal, about a quarter of a mile from the Rhine. Here we hauled the boat ashore, and after supper went on a voyage of discovery to find a carpenter, whom we set to work immediately to make a new set of elbows after the pattern of those which had been shattered by the collision.

At four o'clock the next morning, the carpenter having finished the work given him, we commenced repairing the boat, and the Professor and Captain, with the assistance of the carpenter, worked away during the greater part of the day, the Doctor being occupied in the very useful employment of making nails out of copper wire, and ruffs from the sheet copper. We were surrounded by numbers of

HARD AT WORK.

the villagers, as well as by a strong detachment of small boys, whose services proved very acceptable in the course of the afternoon.

It was certainly not a little annoying to be brought thus to a stand-still in our voyage. Having passed so many other difficulties without injury—huge rafts of timber, locks without end, and barges by the dozen,—here we were, smashed by the last of these, and that just in sight of the Rhine. But we worked right earnestly, and after all did not lose much time. By four o'clock, P.M., the repairs of the boat were finished, and she was ready to be put into the water again, when we met with a further delay, which cost the Professor some little trouble.

The carpenter we had employed had evidently pleased himself with the idea that he should make a good thing of his job, and modestly demanded fifteen francs for his day's work, whilst a companion of his who had provided us with about two pennyworth of copper wire, desired four francs. Robert, the carpenter, after a deal of altercation, came down to eight francs, the Professor still offering him five for his share; and as there appeared to be no chance of settling the matter amicably, without reference to an umpire, he proposed to bring the matter before the Mayor of Kembs, and abide by his decision. Away they went, therefore, in search of his worship, and were soon joined by the carpenter's wife, who was evidently determined to uphold the cause of her lord.

The village mayor, a plain rustic in sabots, finished feeding his pigs, washed his hands, and sat in state. The Professor opened the debate by a plain statement of facts, almost every one of which the carpenter's wife flatly denied. As she waxed warm with the subject, and became very noisy, it was proposed to send her for other witnesses, but the Mayor did not deem this at all necessary, and after an hour's palaver (during which time his worship had taken voluminous notes, and added up interminable figures), recommended the Professor to pay six francs fifty centimes, a sum that he very readily handed over to the workmen; for not to mention the great decrease from their charges, which amounted to nineteen francs, the joke was well worth the money.

While this was going on, a party of gentlemen, and custom house officials who had heard of our arrival, drove up in a carriage and pair, and having alighted, commenced a minute inspection of the boat; one of the officers suspected the Captain of

STATE OF THE RIVER.

being a desperate character, 'for,' said he, 'look at that dangerous weapon he wears at his side,' pointing to the clasp knife that the Captain invariably wore. One of the natives, however, endeavoured to allay his fears, by assuring him that we did not appear to be at all vicious, and that he had seen us using such knives at our luncheon, which we had agreed in the morning should be sent to us from the hotel. They asked us if we at all knew the nature of our undertaking in trusting ourselves in so small a boat upon the Rhine, and they recommended us by all means to take a pilot, for there were many very large and dangerous rocks in the river, and the stream ran an incredible number of miles in the hour. But we respectfully declined doing anything of the kind, for we knew that had we listened to their advice, we should have got into trouble, everybody there being of course unaccustomed to so light a craft, however well they might know the river; more than this, we doubted if any one could have been persuaded to trust himself in the boat with us.

On the return of the Professor, we loaded the small boys with knapsacks and oars, and shouldering the boat, commenced carrying her towards the Rhine, having divested ourselves of shoes and stockings, and tucked up our unmentionables after the fashion of mud-larks, for we had to walk through a swamp on our way. Our hotel-keeper pluckily laid hold of the bows of the boat, and assisted us the whole of the distance, and the crowd that accompanied us having struck up 'Malbrouck s'en va t'en guerre,' away we marched, forming altogether a rather imposing procession. Our admiring companions did not seem to believe that, after they had warned us of rapids, rocks, whirlpools, and other great dangers, which they said we must inevitably encounter, we were really about to trust ourselves on the Rhine, until they saw us fairly in the boat, and then they exclaimed, 'We grieve to think what will become of you; be assured that if you persist in this your rash attempt, you will never reach Strasburg.' And one old gentleman, who had hitherto been silent, cried out, 'Ah, my dear young friends, you will never see England again.' But we pushed off, and amid hearty cheers, pulled away from them at the rate of ten miles an hour.

We had not gone far, when we noticed a peculiar hissing noise in the water, which we could no ways account for, save that perhaps that was the manner in which the water nymphs of the noble

STORMS NEAR BASLE. 73

river expressed their disapprobation of our conduct;
at times it grew so loud, that it seemed as if the
bottom boards of the boat were cracking, or rather
as if the whole of the bottom of the boat was being
fried in a large frying-pan. We noticed this several
times afterwards, but never so particularly as on
this evening.

As there were evident appearances of a thunder-
storm coming on, we determined on putting in at
Neumburg for the night, and accordingly ran the
boat into the nearest point to the town, which is
distant about a mile from the river bank. When
we had taken the traps out of the boat, we moored
her in a small pool, and left her in charge of a
ferryman, whose hut was close at hand; we then
shouldered the oars and knapsacks, and made away
for the town. Presently we were met by a brace of
gendarmes of a most mediæval cut, who, from
their manner and gesticulations, must have taken
us for brigands at the very least. To be sure, we
had not a very prepossessing appearance, for the
morning's work *at* the boat, and the evening's walk
with the boat (through the above mentioned
swamp), had the effect of imparting very varied tints
to our at all times extraordinary costume; this,
coupled with the wonderful implements we carried,

and our extreme unwillingness to drop them even for one instant, raised suspicion and ire in the heart of the gendarmes, who insisted on taking charge of us as far as the town. In vain did the Professor expostulate, in vain did he endeavour to show that we were a harmless lot. 'Harmless, indeed,' said one of them; 'what do all these weapons mean? why look at this (the boat-hook), you could kill a man with this! you must have that iron spike removed before you enter Neumburg; it shall be returned to you, but it cannot be allowed to remain at the end of that spear. Yes, and those daggers, too (our clasp knives), you must give them up, you must indeed.'* Fortunately, on our way, we met with an individual who understood a little English in addition to his German and French; he read and

---

* This circumstance reminds the writer of something that occurred to him in 1846, whilst making a pedestrian tour with his brother through Northamptonshire. He had just finished making a sketch of the market cross of Irthlingborough, when going in to the bar of the hotel to order luncheon, a little dog which lay on the hearth began to bark. 'Oh!' said the landlord, 'doan't mind him, he allus barks when any suspicious-looking characters comes in.' Once, in walking through Cornwall, he was asked, 'You sell tea, do'ee?' But the fact is that country people in England imagine that any one travelling with a knapsack must necessarily be a *tramp*.

Suspicious Characters.

London John W. Parker & Son, West Strand 1854.

explained our passports to the astonished gendarmes, and by his aid we were released from the clutches of the enemy, and conducted to the White Hart, of which hotel he had spoken in *very* high terms, and of which we afterwards discovered that he was the proprietor. Even he, however, seemed a little anxious about us, for he did not leave us the whole of the evening, until we bid him good night.

During our supper, the storm, which had been gathering for some time, broke with all its fury, we all agreed that we never before saw such continuous lightning for so long together; for two hours and a half it was incessant; the whole atmosphere seemed as one blaze of steel blue flame, casting a most peculiar and unearthly appearance over all the grand range of the Schwartzwald, which was visible down as far as the Höllenthal; while, on the other side of the Rhine, the Vosges mountains were now and then to be seen in their stretch towards Strasburg.

CHAPTER IX.

AM RHEIN.

Am Rhein, am Rhein, da wachsen unsre Reben,
Gesegnet sei der Rhein.

M. CLAUDIUS.

DESPITE the rain,— which had fallen in great quantities during the night, and was still coming down very heavily, — we started off for the boat again, much in the same condition as on the previous evening, the only difference being that our mackintoshes, which we had unrolled and thrown over our shoulders, imparted to us a more dilapidated appearance than we even had before.

The boat, when we reached her, was discovered to be half-full of water from the abundant rain; but for this we were not at all sorry, for the intense heat of the last few days especially had so dried her up that we feared that she might start a timber had the hot weather continued.

To turn her over and throw the water out of her was the work of a very little time, and we soon floated away again, wind and stream in our favour.

By the time we reached Alt Breysach the rain had begun to hold off a little, and while the Professor went ashore to procure some luncheon, we remained on board, admiring alternately the grandeur of the Black Forest, which presented a fine appearance as the light fleecy clouds rolled away from the summit of the mountains, and the old Cathedral, which, standing on an eminence surrounded by the town and by the remains of what were once strong fortifications, seems to keep watch over all the surrounding country.

At Alt Breysach, the stream (or rather that arm of the river that runs past the town, for the whole breadth of the Rhine varies from three to four miles all the way from Neumberg to Strasburg,) becomes narrower, and from either bank a strong jetty runs out some way into the water; a swing bridge of boats being the means of communication between the two. The water, as one might suppose, rushes down between the jetties at a furious pace, and it was very evident to us that some little attention would be necessary on our passing this rapid; in fact it required the utmost precaution on the part of the helmsman throughout this day's voyage, as well as strict attention on the part of the crew; for the river being spread over so much ground, and cut up by innumerable islands and sandbanks, necessarily abounds in rapids and falls of water. This was much more the case than usual at the time that we came down, for the river was much swollen, and therefore the shallows, which were the most dangerous parts of it for us, were more numerous.

Really, in looking back, it does seem wonderful how we got through this part of the river as we did; there can be no doubt but that we had a close run for a capsize several times, which might have terminated most unfortunately, seeing that the Doctor, poor man, was no swimmer.

Lunch, consisting of roast veal, bread, a bottle of wine, cherries, and kirschwasser, costing about ten pence for the three, having been consumed, we

THE WHIRLPOOL.

essayed to pass the straits of Alt Breysach, and for this purpose pulled as directly as possible into the middle of the stream, the force of which was even stronger than we had imagined, for the current laid such hold upon the keel of the boat that it was next to impossible to steer her. Going on in this manner, we did not discover our dangerous position until the boat's stern actually swang round over the edge of a whirlpool, caused by some strong out-work of the jetty, and which was roaring away jovially. The boat was being carried round with her bows up stream, when the Captain shouted, 'Now then, boys, hard away with her all—eyes in the boat—stead - - - y !' And having righted her, we presently shot down between the jetties at the rate of fifteen to eighteen miles an hour, the big waves caused by the rapidity of the current following us close astern, and looking as if they would gladly have swamped us if they could.

It was necessary to keep a continual look-out for 'breakers ahead,' and we were every moment obliged to alter the direction of our course, there being no main channel. Now we are sweeping down a rapid so shallow that we can see the bottom, and rush past the trunk of an old tree, which itself, far from appearing to be stationary, seems as if it was being pulled up against the stream by some invisible power,—now we reach the end of the shallow, and the water is boiling and bubbling about us in all directions, and the sharp crested little waves come rattling against the side of the boat like so many undertakers at work. And again, at another time, when we got into rather deeper water where there was less turmoil, we were able to paddle or even float with the stream.

It was on such a bit of water as this that we were quietly resting on our oars, and enjoying our pipes, the Doctor, as usual, when there was no work to be done, lying at full length in the bows, and the Professor puzzling his brains about the different changes of money we should in all probability meet with, when the Captain, suddenly hearing a much louder noise than was at all ordinary, and standing up, discovered that we were making straight away for a waterfall, about a half mile distant. 'Oars, all!' he cries; 'put your backs into it, and keep her steady whatever you do;' for he was obliged to stand up, that looking well a-head he might determine what course to follow. So, pulling the rudder hard up, and steering for

SHALLOWS. 81

the opposite bank, we managed, after a few dozen strokes, hard pulling, to avoid the fall; although, even then, we were not the boat's length from one end of it. As we swept down another channel, and got a full view of the danger we had escaped, the Professor could not refrain from a shout of mingled pleasure and surprise. Had the boat gone over, she must have been inevitably smashed to pieces, for the fall was one of about ten feet, and there was an immense body of water rushing over at a fearful rate.

The Coxswain was often greatly puzzled to decide which stream to follow, or on which side of an island or sandbank he should steer; and down about the mouth of the Elz, a small river which runs from Freyburg, the shallows were frequent, so that we seemed quite to have entered a maze of them. We were in a fair direction for avoiding one of these shallows, and the Coxswain had, as he thought, a clear run, when another, at a small distance further on, made its appearance; for a moment, he could not think what to be at; there was not space to pull across it as he had managed the first, for had this been attempted, we should have been carried upon the shallow 'broad-side on,' and rolled over and over like a barrel, whilst it would have

G

been madness to have attempted the sheer impossibility of pulling against the stream. So, making the best of a bad matter, he followed the counsel of the Cornishman, who, seeing the lamps of a mail coach coming down hill at a rapid pace, while he in his single gig was ascending, and fancying them both dangerous looking articles, thought the best plan would be 'to draive raight 'twix 'em,' which we did accordingly in regard of the shallows. Fortunately for us, the issue was in our case less disastrous, for he, poor man, was very much injured, and his gig of course smashed to pieces, whilst we, after floating down a little way, only scraped the boat keel along the gravelly bottom, until we gradually came to a stand still. The Professor was going to jump out, when ''Vast a bit,' said the Captain ; ' we shall have some work to get you on board again.' And altering our position in the boat so as to weight her forward, she floated off again, but grated her keel all the way down the shallow.

As there seemed to be no main channel, we had not the most remote idea at times where we were, whether we were near the right or the left bank of the river, or whether the bank that we were passing was that of an island, or of the river itself; but

Passing the Shallows.

London, John W. Parker & Son, West Strand, 1854.

KEHL. 83

this mattered little; we were on the Rhine, we knew, and the Rhine flowed to Strasburg, we thought; we were not then aware that that city is distant a mile and a half from the river.

After numerous other scrapes and dodgings about from one side to the other, sometimes whizzing past the banks, which often had the same appearance as when one looks out of a railway train in motion on an adjoining hedge, at others sweeping down a broad piece of water, which looked (as it really was) like a large inclined plane, and again at other times, pulling against a bit of back-water, we at length arrived at Kehl, having come over no less than seventy miles of ground in six hours and a quarter, exclusive of the halt we made at Alt Breysach. On hauling the boat into a timber-yard, near the bridge at Kehl, the Doctor made the remark, that he doubted if the crew of the 'Water Lily' had even on the Danube met with such continuously rapid and dangerous streams, or had attained the speed that the 'Undine' had on that day ; and we congratulated ourselves on our arrival here, spite of all our friends at Kembs had told us, and thought it a favourable omen that perhaps we might see England again after all.

Leaving the boat at Kehl, we took our knap-

G 2

sacks, and walked over to Strasburg, and astonished the military at the Porte d'Austerlitz, by shouting as we entered,

> O Strasbourg! O Strasbourg!
> Du wunderschöne stadt
> Darinnen liegt begraben
> Ein mannicher soldat, &c., &c.

One of the first things we did on reaching the town, was to give our canvas shoes a coat of pipe-clay, for by this time they had become very grey. The sun had also affected ourselves as well as our clothing in no small degree. Both the Professor and the Doctor were marked with a line round the neck of a deep copper colour, which at a distance might have led one to suppose that they once had their heads cut off, and then skilfully replaced. During our first stroll along the streets, we saw a travelling doctor, whose principal occupation seemed to be drawing teeth (his victims being compelled to mount his large travelling carriage in full view of the crowd) to the sound of three vile musicians, who accompanied him; and holding forth to the people on the virtues of his infallible medicines. It was highly amusing to witness the different expressions on the faces of the poor

STRASBURG.

wretches who placed themselves under the power of his muscular arm.

The dresses of the peasants, too, who were absorbed in attention to this wonderful doctor (whose house, as he told them, was the largest in all Paris), were some of them very peculiar, those from the other side of the river being by far the most picturesque. The men wear a stiff black felt hat, with one half the brim turned up; a long frock coat, the waist of which appears between the shoulder blades; a highly embroidered waistcoat; plush tights, and boots reaching the knee.

The peculiar part of female attire is the large bow of wide black ribbon, which is worn on the top of the head without cap or bonnet, and a small shawl round the neck, the longer end of which hangs down in front instead of behind. But we must leave this interesting scene, for we hear it hinted that we belong to the same party as the gentleman with the large house.

Of course we visited the Cathedral, whose spire is the highest in the world, being more than twenty feet higher than the great pyramid of Egypt, and whose west window is higher than the *towers* of York Minster. Of course we saw the wonderful clock, and admired the fine organ and the inimitable stained glass; but except the Cathedral there is not much to interest in Strasburg.

When we returned to Kehl we found that the boat had been well taken care of; and in a short time, our arrival having been made known in the barracks, a complete regiment of soldiers, officers and *douaniers*, had collected to see us start. The water was too high, and the current too strong, to admit of our shooting the bridge, so, carrying the boat across the road, we launched her on the other side, and pulled away amid the cheers of our martial beholders.

The navigation below Strasburg is much more simple, the water deeper, the channel easy to be distinguished, and the current by no means as strong as above the city; thus we were able to take it very quietly, and floated with the stream during most of the day, having shipped the oars and allowing the current to take us where it would, for our civilized life of two days at Strasburg had made us feel rather disinclined for work. In the evening we stopped at a small auberge near Lauterbourg, where there is a frontier of some sort; we therefore fraternized with the *douaniers*, whom we found to be very civil, and afterwards had an interesting chat with the landlord about America, he having resided some time in New Orleans with his wife and child.

We had pulled in here only just in time to avoid another smart storm, and were more than delighted to return once again to our semi-bargee style of life.

The next day, Sunday, we staid on board, floating towards Mannheim on the broad bosom of the mighty river. With a beautifully bright sun above us and an atmosphere cooled by last night's rain, everything looked fresh and happy. No one could have mistaken that morning for any other morning of the week; for from the quiet appearance of the sky, and the earth, and the trees, and the cattle, one would have declared that it was Sunday, such an air of rest pervaded everything—save the river,— but even this having now collected itself into one broad stream, swells in silent majesty onwards in its course towards the ocean. So profoundly quiet did everything seem, that when we no longer broke the silence with our voices, not a sound fell on the ear, even of a ripple against the boat side. Now and then, perhaps, we should hear the splash of some fish which had risen above the water in pursuit of its prey, or the faint booming of some distant church bell; but beyond these all was stillness. It proved so thoroughly enjoyable during the whole of the day, that we were not tempted to land once; we did not even visit the Cathedral of Speyer, which, we understood, had lately undergone extensive restorations. Between Philipsburg and Mannheim there are many artificial cuttings, through which the greater part of the stream now flows, and these being more direct than the original bed of the river, the distance is much shortened.

On reaching Mannheim in the evening, we shot the bridge of boats, to the delight and astonishment of those who happened to be crossing, as well as many other persons on the banks of the river. It was rather amusing too, being compelled to introduce a hitherto unknown phrase in boating, for the bridges are so low that we were obliged to lie flat in the boat whilst passing under, to avoid a blow which would otherwise peril our heads. The Captain was wont therefore to give his orders—'Ship—Duck!'—which were as promptly obeyed. It was not always that we could shoot these bridges, some of them, like one we passed to-day at Rhein-bad, being so very low that we were compelled to lift the boat out and carry her over.

We stopped just outside the Hôtel de l'Europe,

MANNHEIM. 89

and the proprietor in ecstacy informed us that 'this was the two English boat that have here been;' in allusion, no doubt, to the first 'Water Lily,' the performance of her crew having left a wonderful impression on the minds of the good folks of Mannheim, although the stories they tell about her are sometimes scarcely credible; for instance, we were informed that she was no thicker than paper, and that it had only taken her crew little more than an hour to row from Mannheim to Heidelberg, a distance of twelve miles, against a strong current.

The hotel keeper paid us every attention, took us to see the 'Bier Keller' (where we discovered from two to three hundred people of all classes unanimously occupied in imbibing beer), and amused us in the course of the evening by telling us how much beer a Bavarian can drink at a sitting, and how many barrels of beer were consumed every Sunday at the 'Keller.'

CHAPTER X.

HEIDELBERG—A SCHLAGER FECHT.

> Lied der Lieder, hall'es wieder:
> Gross und deutsch sei unsre Muth.
> Seht hier den geweihten Degen,
> Thut, wie brave Burschen pflegen
> Und durchbohrt den freien Hut!
>
> Seht ihn blinken in den Linken,
> Diesen Schläger, nie entweiht
> Ich durchbohr' den Hut und schwöre,
> Halten will Ich stets auf Ehre,
> Stets ein braver Bursche sein.

E had stowed the boat for the night in the same stable that the 'Water Lily,' during her sojourn at Mannheim, had used for a boathouse; and in the morning the waiters, &c., of the Hôtel de l'Europe, being somewhat too gentlemanly, in their own opinion, to lend a hand in carrying the boat to the water, we shouldered her ourselves, to the surprise of the Kelner, who seemed to think that the least that we could have done would have been to have hired four porters for the purpose. The flood gates of the canal, which here joins the Rhine with the Neckar by a short cut, were closed, owing to the great height of the water in the former river ; we therefore pulled down to the mouth of the Neckar, and once more commenced work against stream.

Near the suspension bridge, which carries the main road to Groszsachsen, we discovered a small steamer ready to start for Heidelberg ; we therefore commenced a race with her, and after pulling away for about a quarter of an hour, we had drawn ahead of her ; but of course we had put on a pace that we could not keep up for any length of time, so we laid on our oars, and dropped astern again. The few passengers ·on board the steamer wished us very much to renew the race, and endeavour to overtake them, but we respectfully declined, for we found the stream getting much stronger as we advanced. In fact, we had as great difficulty in pulling through the railway bridge at Ladenberg, as we formerly had at Melun. There are very frequent shallows in this river also, for being small it has been found necessary to make an artificial channel, by partially filling up some parts of the stream, and running out banks of stone in others; for before this was done, it was impossible for the smallest steamer to navigate the river, which is now, however, rendered accessible as far as Heilbronn. The steamers they use are small, flat-bottomed boats, which often touch the ground on their course, and sometimes come to a stand still altogether; but when stemming the current where it happens to be rather swifter than usual, it becomes necessary to assist the paddles by the use of long poles, and punt the boat up the stream.

We very often came upon rocks in our course to Heidelberg, and the Captain and Professor had frequently to jump out, and lift the boat off, or rather over them; and sometimes to take her by the bows, and walk her up a shallow.

Arriving at Heidelberg, we eschewed the town itself as a resting place, and remained on the opposite bank of the river, the Professor having discovered a very comfortable gasthof, with the sign, "Zum silberner Anker.' The landlord, as hearty an old fellow as ever breathed, accompanied the

Captain in the course of the evening with a cornet, while he played on a small harmonium belonging to the house.

The next morning we were glad to have the first news from England, for we had not as yet received any communication since we started. We also found our friends B. and P., who had arrived before us, and had been expecting us for the last few days; they accompanied us over the glorious old castle, as also the town (which, by the bye, has a very 'varsity look about it), came and dined with us, and then, the Professor endeavouring to show us that it was our duty not to waste time, or stay any longer at Heidelberg, we packed up our few things, much to the regret of the Doctor. The Captain suddenly became poorly; looked as if he had great difficulty in digesting his late meal ; had not much to say to anybody ; but commenced, as was his wont when anything went wrong, throwing pebbles into the water, watching the result as earnestly as if he were endeavouring to solve some unaccountable natural phenomenon, and when this process is completed, he stalks off with his hands thrust into his pockets, and an air of 'I'm blowed if I'll pay the taxes' about him. But soon resuming his cheerful mood (owing, no doubt, to the fact of his dinner having been by this time properly digested, he cries, 'All right! come along, old fellows,' and the boat is launched, and we are off again. We had gone some way down the river, when the Professor discovered that he had lost his favourite tobacco pouch. The Captain was landed to search for it at the gasthof, and in his absence the Doctor worked very hard on the feelings of the Professor to induce him to return for another night. He was successful in this endeavour, for the Captain soon descried the 'Undine' returning; nor did he mind being charged with—for, in fact, it would have been difficult for him to deny—having wilfully hidden the pouch in order that we might have another day at Heidelberg. However, it was a very good thing eventually, for we should have missed one of the most pleasant days of our trip, had we left on that evening; beyond this, the Professor's usual method of extreme anxiety to get to a place, and, the moment he has reached it, his extreme anxiety to get out of it again, was broken into, and that amicably; for he was a person of great weight and authority, seeing that he had entire control of the needful, and might not therefore well be offended.

Our landlord's delight at our return was very

great, he called us his dear sons, and said he knew we must come back again ; he embraced us after the fashion of an ursal hug, and in order to prevent us from again leaving, he seized our knapsacks, and carried them off to his own room, so that we were compelled to sit in boating costume all the evening. We could not comprehend all this affection at the time, but when our friends B. and P. joined us again in the evening, B. was told in confidence by the landlord, that he had two brothers in France who were making their fortunes, and that he and his wife were talking the matter over last night, and had come to this conclusion, that we were his nephews come over *incog.* to find out how he fared in the world, and that when he saw us that afternoon returning, was more convinced of this than ever. We kept up the joke as well as we were able, though our good host was not a little mystified to find us talking English rather than German, in addition to what he considered to be our native tongue—viz., French, of which language, however, he did not know a single word.

We were visited by some Oxford men, who were living in the Schloss—a reading party for the long vacation—and their coach, an old Oxford stroke, appeared very highly delighted at the unexpected rencontre.

The Captain now went to call on an English family, with whom he was acquainted, and asked the ladies to come and see the boat on the following morning; on his return, he found his crew with their friends discussing dinner, again, as the Professor thought, previous to our departure. But having first joined in the chorus—

> Edite, bibite collegiales
> Post multa sæcula pocula nulla—

the Captain mentioned his engagement for the morning, and he could hardly distinguish which was most marked, the Doctor's delight at a still further sojourn at Heidelberg, or the Professor's disgust at the same.

In the course of the evening, the Captain and Doctor sung some few German songs, 'Scheiden,' 'Was kommt dort von der Höh' (of which there is a translation in 'Hyperion'), 'Treue Liebe,' and some others, which they had previously learnt in England; and the old aubergier was really at his wit's end. 'Ach, ihr schlauen füchse!' cried he; 'you have told me all along that you could not speak German, and now you sing the very songs that are most familiar to me, and you have under-

HEIDELBERG—THE SCHLOSS.

stood all that I have said, and would not answer me. Dass ist nicht schön von Ihnen !' Our friends, however, endeavoured to pacify him, by telling him that we really did not speak German. B. and P. left us, declaring that if we spent many such pleasant evenings as that, we must indeed have 'a jolly time of it.'

Next morning, unfortunately, it was raining hard ; in fact we had experienced heavy showers for the last two days, and as the German proverb says, 'Heidelberg is a pleasant place when it has done raining.' The ladies, however, were bold enough to encounter the rain, and though we could not give them a cruise in the boat, we pulled about a little in front of the town, and they expressed their delight and astonishment at the size of the boat, which they said was so small for so long a voyage. But they were more pleased at the sight of the British colours at our bows, than anything else. As it continued to rain, we all visited the Castle again, and went over the Museum, which we had omitted to see on our former visit. It is not, as it purports to be, a collection entirely of things found on the Castle, but a private speculation, containing curiosities from many quarters, some few of the articles having been found on the spot.

H

Made a second cruise with an Englishman, whose name we had not yet learned; and a smart shower coming on, got thoroughly drenched; though, of course, we, being in flannels, did not feel the bad effect of the same so much as he did. On our return, we were joined by the English cleric of the place, who, after several compliments, said he wished that we could instil the love of boating into some of the German students, in the hope that eventually they might take more interest in that pastime than in drinking beer and duelling.

We spent the evening with our English friends, and the Captain was surprised and much pleased to see a piece of stone carving that had been brought from England,—the handiwork of a younger brother; and before we left, S. asked us to accompany him in the morning to witness a duel, which he understood was to take place at the Red Fisherman's.

Now these *schläger fechte* are utterly forbidden by the government, and a large reward offered to the police on the detection of anything of the kind; but the amount of this reward being doubled by the various clubs of students, to induce the police to keep out of the way, they are rarely discovered. Now and then perhaps, when some poor

HEIDELBERG—A SCHLÄGER FECHT. 99

unfortunate freshmen are rash enough to enter the lists, the police pounce upon them in the midst of their work ; and as it is seldom that any others than freshmen are caught, it has been hinted that information concerning ' the whereabouts' has been previously sent to the police by no less a person than the president of the fight himself; just, as it were, to keep the thing going.

There are numerous clubs, whose members, however, are not confined to the University of Heidelberg, and for the sake of distinction they assume the name of different parts of Germany, though it is no more necessary that a man should be a native of any particular state, the name of which his club has assumed, than it is necessary to be a fishmonger to belong to the honourable Company of Fishmongers in England; but before a man is even eligible to these clubs, he must have fought a certain number of duels, or be able to drink a certain quantity of beer at a sitting. Concerning the consumption of that fluid, they have numberless regulations, which vary with the clubs; the rules of one allowing its members to have two pulls at a pint, while those of another do not permit that a glass once filled should be set down again until it is emptied. All this beer-

H 2

drinking, added to the quantity of tobacco they smoke, imparts to most of the men (although some may have strong constitutions enough to bear it) a very washed-out appearance. They would certainly want long training before they could stand work in an eight-oar, much less compete with a crew of water-rats, as they call the English. Their constant practice with the *schläger* undoubtedly gives them a quick eye and square shoulders (the latter painfully so), but it also has an unfortunate effect of disfiguring the face to a great degree. This disfigurement is, however, among themselves, held in great repute; much on the principle, we suppose, of Scotch terrier beauty; for they consider a man looks all the more noble in proportion to the number of scars he has on his face. The members of the different clubs are distinguished by different coloured caps, and duellists wear in addition a small thin sash across the breast, also bearing the colour of the club.* The Professor was bold enough to wear a sky blue cap he had brought with him, and evidently puzzled many a student to discover to

---

* The colour of the club which is composed entirely of students in Theology, is black; of students in Philosophy, green; and of students in Law, blue.

HEIDELBERG—A SCHLÄGER FECHT. 101

what club he belonged, for it much resembled in shape the ordinary club cap.

At nine o'clock in the morning our friend S—— called and informed us that a duel was certainly going to take place, for he saw the women on the look out; and walking along the riverside, we observed three or four women sitting down at intervals by the side of the road, knitting, but having near them an umbrella each, to be used as a telegraphic signal on the approach of any hostile police-officer, who, as I said before, is seldom to be found on these occasions. A walk of ten minutes brought us to the house of the red fisherman, a brawny old fellow of sixty, who takes care of the bandages and sharpens the swords for most of the clubs. Mounting the stairs, we were ushered into an ordinary sized apartment, furnished with small tables and benches, at which there were numbers of students sitting, and even at that early hour were smoking, drinking coffee or liqueurs, and playing cards or dice. In the centre of the room two men were being bandaged to a vast extent. All the front part of the body is covered with a thick pad, girt at the waist by a wide band, which at the same time serves to keep in its place a sort of pillow to fit into the hollow of the back; the throat is next bandaged in a most surgical manner, and the sword-arm of each man is also padded to such a degree that it becomes necessary for the second to assist him by carrying it about for him as soon as the pad is adjusted; a small cap, with an iron peak to protect the eyes, completes the costume. As soon as both the combatants were dressed for the fight, we all moved into an adjoining hall; at one end of which, and on opposite sides of it, the combatants take their position, each being attended by a couple of seconds, the duty of one being to stand by his man to ward off false blows and the like (and he seemed to have as much work, and to require almost a quicker eye than those actually engaged), and the other to take charge of the sword-arm, to arrange the dress, and to replace the weapon by another in case of a fracture.

The president of the fight, a small, thin, though well-made man, with a less number of scars than most of the men, next took up his position in the centre of the hall, and seeing that all was ready, shouted, 'Silentium!' In an instant there was a dead silence, and the combatants might be observed panting with excitement; whether they were also 'eager for the fray,' is another question. *Fertig! loss!* cries one of the seconds, and they rush in

Fertig — los.

London, John W. Parker & Son, West Strand, 1854.

HEIDELBERG—A SCHLÄGER FECHT. 103

upon one another and clash their swords together some three or four strokes, when one of the seconds interposes his sword, and crying ' Halt !' retires with his man to have his sword straightened, or to give him rest, as the case may be. Again they cry *Fertig! loss!* and again, after a few passes are made, they retire, this is repeated a third time, when the President gives leave for a little rest, and the combatants walk up and down the hall, each having his arm carried horizontally for him, and each man panting with excitement and exertion; for as it has been said before, the pads and bandages are very heavy.

It appeared to us that one of the most frequent, and therefore we supposed the principal stroke aimed at, was to strike your sword low down, perhaps four inches from the handle upon your adversary's bandaged arm, so that the end of the weapon (the only part that is sharpened) should *flick* itself in against your opponent's face.

' Silentium!' is again called, and going to work with renewed vigour, the Hanoverian receives a gash on the left nostril. He is led up to the President, who, on measuring the wound, finds that it is not of sufficient length or depth to decide the battle; the combat is therefore once more renewed; but now they fight with more energy than ever, and the Suabian breaks his sword, the broken end whizzing over to the other end of the room, and perilling the eyes of the bystanders. At length, after another rest and a few more attacks or *rounds*, as perhaps we should call them, the president cries, *Halt!* and the fight is over, twenty minutes having elapsed, which is the full amount of time allowed for giving and receiving satisfaction. If at first he who considered himself insulted had challenged his man to fight him for an inch only, this battle would have been concluded when the Hanoverian was wounded, but he considered himself aggrieved to the length of two inches, and half an inch deep. And this is the rule, that according to the magnitude of the insult, so great must the wound be, and sometimes, though not often, the combat is mortal.

We had seen quite enough of this sort of thing, so capping our company, we left them to fight out about half a dozen more battles in the same way; but how many more were on that day similarly beautified, we never learnt.

It seems quite as unintelligible to the German student how we rub on together at our Universities without quarrelling, as their practice of thus dis-

HEIDELBERG—A SCHLÄGER FECHT. 105

figuring themselves for life seems absurd to us. They say that if we, the English, do not have a fight occasionally, we must go and sulk it out, which is much worse; but these men get up a duel on the slightest provocation.

Yet for all this, there are many men who go through their course of lectures in a quiet and reasonable manner. It is only 'the old ones,' 'the princes of twilight,' who indulge in these quaint and curious pastimes.

CHAPTER XI.

MOSQUITOES AND WORMS.

HΛΕ. Ὦ πασᾶν κείνα πλέον ἀμέ-
ρ᾽ ἐλθοῦσ᾽ ἐχθίστα δή μοι·
Ὦ νύξ, ὦ δείπνων ἀρρήτων
Ἔκπαγλ᾽ ἄχθη·
Electra.

OUR worthy old host, on our return to the gasthof, evidently saw that we were determined to leave this time, and expressed his deep regret at the same; and when we were about to start presented us with a quantity of tobacco in the leaf, the product of his own garden, and also a bottle of wine from his own vineyard.

He brought out his cornet and made the hills re-echo the martial tunes 'Die alte Krieger,' and 'Was blasen die Trompeten,' and we left Heidelberg not without many regrets on all hands, and floated down the Neckar till the sounds of the cornet died in the distance.

It did not take us long to reach Mannheim again, though we were obliged to be careful as to our course, for the river abounds in rocks, the sight of which alarmed our English acquaintance (who took a cruise with us in the rain yesterday, and had agreed to accompany us to-day as far as Mannheim), for he had surreptitiously taken off his shoes, and coat also, that he might be prepared to swim in case of a capsize, of which, however, there was not much danger. The Doctor and our friend were equally astonished, while talking on English matters, to find that they had known each other in London some two years ago; but the alteration of their visages (both having discarded the use of the razor) was so great that they had not hitherto recognised one another.

We parted at Mannheim, and, once more floating down the Rhine, for it was very hot weather, we soon sighted Worms; but not being at all desirous of stopping here, we pulled on to Gernsheim, near which place we took up our quarters for the night at a small house by the river side. After supper we retired to our bedroom, but not to rest, for the mosquitoes, which had, even during supper time, attacked the Doctor, really swarmed in the sleeping apartment. We 'laid us down and closed our eyes,' but all our attempts to sleep were quite hopeless, so we got up and put on our clothes again, and in order to cover every part of the body we were obliged to use our socks, which had to be pulled out of the knapsacks, for we had long ago given up wearing them; in fact, the greater part of the day it was our custom, generally, to go without shoes either. But the worrying little insects penetrated even these. We tried all sorts of ways to avoid these horrible little things, for the irritation arising from the punctures they make in the flesh was almost intolerable. Getting out of bed again, we put on our mackintoshes, and, walking up and down the apartment, endeavoured to disperse them by creating a dense cloud of tobacco smoke; but they seemed delighted at this, and we had to keep our temper as well as we were able, smoking our pipes to the music of their everlasting *bizz*. At length the Doctor, having muffled himself in jerseys, shirts, and anything he could

A warm night near Gersheim.

London: John W. Parker & Son, West Strand, 1854.

lay hold of, rolls about in agony upon the floor; the Captain, longing for the daylight to make its appearance, wrings his hands in the bitterness of anguish; while from the bed of the Professor, to which he has retired, a semi-swinelike grunt may ever and anon be heard, as some unhappy tormentor inserts its proboscis into the cuticle of that worthy.

We went out in the early morning for a bathe, to try to alleviate the pain arising from the bites of the mosquitoes, but it was not of much service; and in the course of the day, what with the heat of the sun and the intense irritation, the hands and faces both of the Doctor and Professor, were covered with blotches as if they had been attacked with the small pox, although this natural and artificial phenomenon was indubitably aggravated by the constant rubbing and scratching with which they increased the irritation.

We reached Mayence in the heat of the day, and having stowed the boat away, left the Professor in charge, and started by rail for Frankfort to procure letters &c. we expected to find there. The English Consul, upon whom we called, was much interested in the account of our excursion, and ran into a long story of a scheme he once had for bringing vessels from London to Frankfort direct, by giving them a shifting keel, to be used at sea but removed on entering the river; but from the model he showed us, we should very much doubt the practicability of the scheme. He also told us that he had been the means of establishing a direct communication by barge from Cologne to the Black Sea; moreover, he had, he said, been very instrumental in bringing the Queen of England on her visit to the Rhine some years ago, having first started the notion, and having procured at his own expense all the soundings of the river. That was the first time he had heard of the appearance of the British standard on the Rhine, and this was the first time he had heard of the union-jack on the same river. He much regretted that we had not brought the boat to Frankfort, and wondered to learn that we had carried the British colours right through France, 'without any squabbles or fuss. Only Englishmen,' said he, getting enthusiastic, 'would have originality to form or pluck to carry out such an undertaking.'

We returned to Mayence, or rather to Castel, in the evening, and the following morning, having spent a few hours in looking over the Cathedral, &c., of Mayence, left on our way to Rudesheim. When

Making the best of it.

London. John W. Parker & Son, West Strand. 1854.

we had reached Eltville, a thunder-cloud having broken just over us, we pulled ashore on the opposite bank of the river, and lighting a fire (for the wind coming down from the mountains was blowing rather strong and very cold), we lay down alongside and proceeded to discuss our mid-day meal, which consisted of two courses of cold meat, with vegetables (we longed to be near a potatoe field, as we had a fire), bottle of wine, ditto beer, a little pastry, or something in the shape of sizings, cherries *ad libitum*, and kirschwasser, which last was with us the Latin for cold veal, on the same principle as brandy is the Latin for roast goose in England, though it is difficult to discover the wit or the sense of the saying; but perhaps neither is intended.

As we successively reached Hattenheim and Giesenheim, two small places on the right bank of the river, we landed for an inspection of the villages, and near the latter we met an English family who occupied a small château by the side of the river, having the famous Johannisberger vineyards at the back of the house. After some conversation with the inmates, we endeavoured to persuade the ladies to join us for a small cruise; but on their declining, we left them, paddling on till we reached Rudesheim.

In the same hotel at which we stopt there was a wandering school out for the vacation. This is a very capital arrangement, and it is a great pity that such a plan is not followed up in England.

During the summer holidays, all the boys who are by the wish of their friends to remain for that time under the care of the master, and as many other boys of the school as may wish to join them, start for a pedestrian trip from town to town, under the charge of one or two ushers, or perhaps the master himself.

Each boy is provided with a small knapsack and a walking stick, and the whole party trudge quietly on, making perhaps from six to nine miles a day; it being an understood thing that innkeepers lodge and provide for the whole party at a much lower rate than for each separately. Some of these boys were English, and one told us that his parents lived in Ceylon. They seemed a happy lot of little fellows, and were no doubt enjoying their holiday as much as we were.

We walked down to Ehrenfels, went over the ruins of the castle, had a good view of the Bingenloch, Maus-thurm, and Bingen, with the mouth of the river Nahe, and returned through the vineyards in the evening

A PROFESSOR.

As we were preparing to start (the Doctor assisting the Captain in sponging out the boat, a piece of work which was as regularly performed as the process of 'swabbing decks' on board ship), we were accosted by a professor of languages, who resided at Bingen. He presented a very dilapidated appearance, and first addressed himself to the Doctor, who, without looking at him, answered—

'Ich verstehe nicht Deutsch.'

'But I to you spik Engleesch,' replied the man.

'Oh! indeed. I beg your pardon.'

'Yehs. You go to Bingen? I will mit you to Bingen drive, since quickly you will drive in your boat.'

'Unfortunately, we are not going to Bingen, you see,' said the Doctor.

'Ah!' replied he, 'you must go; dare are manny Inglis peebls dar!'

'Why, the fact is, we wish to get on this morning, and have no time for Bingen; besides you know we can see English people anywhere.'

'So you get on?' said he, evidently much disappointed at not being able to take a drive with us. But turning to the Captain he put the question—

'Are you one famille? or will man discover?'

This was rather a stumper; but imagining the meaning of it to be, 'are you all of one family—a party travelling for pleasure, or are you on a voyage of discovery,' we informed him of the nature of our expedition, which, however, after much explanation he failed to understand. And while he was again expressing his regret that he could not 'with us to Bingen drive,' we pulled away from Rudesheim and its inhabitants, who had all turned out to see us with our English temerity attempt the passage of the Bingen-loch.

We could not but give a glance of pity towards Bingen, as we thought of the poor unfortunates who had placed themselves under the tutorship of our literary friend for the purpose of learning English.

As we passed the Maus-Thurm we met a large steam-tug, with six or seven barges astern, slowly struggling her way up stream. She, of course, created some little disturbance in the water, and, although we were knocked about a good deal, pulled past them all without shipping any water; in fact, we were rather disappointed than otherwise, that the dreaded passage of the Bingen-loch was so very easy, for certainly from the great talk

THE BINGEN-LOCH. 115

we had heard about it, we expected something more. But the rapidity of the current, or roughness of the stream, though of course much increased by the steamer, was not for one moment to be compared with what we had previously met above Strasburg; though at the same time we could not help thinking that it must have been a very superior breed of rats that swam the river at this point, on their way to make a meal of the far-famed Bishop Hatto.

The Professor was so much disappointed in the passage of the Bingen-loch, that he wished to try how close we could go, without being capsized, to a rock in the centre of the river just above Lorch, and upon which a barge had drifted, the water at the time we passed making a clean breach over her.

I 2

CHAPTER XII.

BINGEN TO COLOGNE.

O the pride of the German heart in this noble river!
And right it is, for of all the rivers of this beautiful earth,
there is none so beautiful as this. There is hardly a league
of its whole course, from its cradle in the snowy Alps, to
its grave in the sands of Holland, which boasts not its
peculiar charms. By heaven, if I were a German, I would
be proud of it too; and of the clustering grapes that hang
about its temples as it reels onwards through vineyards
in a triumphant march, like Bacchus crowned and drunken.
—*Hyperion.*

AFTER passing Lorch, we pulled ashore under the ruins of Fürstenburg for a bathe, and seemed more than ever to enjoy our mode of travelling; we could land where we liked and stop when we pleased, not being tied to time for anything; on the contrary, so

OBERWESEL. 117

little was this the case, that we rarely apportioned ourselves a day's work, or knew in the morning where we should stop in the evening. In fact we never considered this last point settled till we had hauled the boat ashore for the night.

Floating down past Bacharach and Kaub, we stopped to dine near Oberwesel, and while the Doctor and Professor took their noontide siesta, the Captain made a small excursion into the country to obtain a view of the river from the summit of the adjacent hills.

To attempt a description of this or any other part of the Rhine through which we passed, would be only absurd in such a mere log-book as the present. This has been often done already by many far abler pens than the Captain's; for not to mention Schiller, Byron, or Longfellow's beautiful allusions to the noble river, or those of a number of prose writers, there is scarce a guide-book to the Rhine which does not abound in the most glowing accounts of the delightful and varied scenery, or in recitals of the many legends attached to every ruin, rock, and road-side cross that one continually meets with. It might safely be said, beyond all this, that the Rhine is better known, even by Englishmen, than most of our own lakes and rivers, seeing it is calculated that about one million of our own countrymen travel yearly upon the stream.

There is a facetious echo at Oberwesel, by which the curious inquirer on asking the question—What is the mayor of Oberwesel? is informed (in German of course) *esel*, that is, an ass. It must be rather an unhappy thing for the townspeople to have thus invariably an ass at their head.

As we passed down, the water was flowing over the petrified remains of the seven cruel countesses of Schönberg, who, as the legend says, were turned into rocks for being unfaithful to their devoted suitors. Near this place we overtook a gentleman belonging to St. Goar, who was also going down the stream in a small ship-shape boat of his own construction; we entered into conversation with him, and on passing the Lurlei-felsen, he pointed out a part of the rock which much resembled the physiognomy of poor Louis-Philippe. We got over the terrible whirlpool of Lurlei called the Gewirr without danger, and after pulling over one or two ebullitions of water near what is called 'the bank' (a part of the river not quite so deep as the rest), pulled on to St. Goar. We were fated to be disappointed, however, as much here as at the Bingen-loch, for even here, where we were told there was such a dangerous whirlpool, it did not effect us as much as many another one above Strasburg. It is true that the large rafts that float down the Rhine were increasing in their onward course, are often, in passing the Lurlei, half carried under water by the violence of the current; but it is evident that to so light a craft as ours there would be no chance of anything of the kind, for she would easily skim over a part of the river that might be dangerous for a boat of larger dimensions, or for anything that drew more water.

We could not resist stopping at St. Goar to visit the extensive ruin of Rheinfels, 'magnificent in its appearance, and interesting from its history, rewarding the trouble of an ascent by the view it commands.' The original edifice was constructed by one who rejoiced in the euphonious title of Diether von Katzenellenbogen, (cat's elbow.)

At Boppard we met with a very spirited reception; so much so, that we were constrained to carry the boat into the stable of the hotel, to avoid the chance of her being pulled to pieces by the anxious endeavours of the public to ascertain how, and of what material, she was constructed. We visited the large convent of Marienburg, 'built in 1738, behind Boppard, once a cotton mill, afterwards a girl's school, and now converted into a medical boarding-house for the water cure.' From our bedroom we looked out on the castles of Sternberg and Liebenstein, called from their picturesqueness, and the tale of their former owners, 'The Brothers,' who having fallen in love with the same fair damsel, settled the matter in the Kilkenny cat fashion, and killed each other.

Next morning a very easy pull brought us to Stolzenfels, and we ran ashore at Kapellen, a small village at the foot of the hill on which the castle stands. We were well rewarded for the trouble of ascending the hill, for the castle has been restored in a right royal fashion, being now the country seat of the King of Prussia. It contains many remarkably good pre-Raphaelite pictures, and the Rittersaal is painted in fresco by M. Stilke, of Dusseldorf. The view from the castle turret is very fine and extensive, reaching upwards as far as Braubach and Marxburg, and downwards a long way past Coblentz, the fortress of Ehrenbreitstein forming a grand feature in this view, whilst immediately opposite it is the mouth of the Lahn, the picturesque village of Nieder Lahnstein, and the ruins of Lahneck. This whole scene was to us rendered much more

COBLENTZ. 121

imposing by the sudden approach of a heavy thunder cloud against the otherwise bright sky. The commanding position of this most noble of the feudal castles of the Rhine quite justifies the name it has received—viz., Proud Rock; but the dignity of the place must have suffered considerably when (as really was the case not long before its restoration) it was offered for sale at seventy dollars, and did not even then find a purchaser.

We walked into Coblentz in the afternoon, and on our way met several young peasant girls, wearing very richly embroidered head-dresses, with a stiletto, or rather imitation paper-knife, of silver gilt, stuck through the hair at the back. This custom also prevails in Belgium, among the unmarried peasants, but they add huge earrings, with diamonds invariably set in gold, and sometimes a plate of silver gilt covers the forehead.

Of course we could do nothing less than visit what we had time for in Coblentz, and also the fortification, rock, and fortress of Ehrenbreitstein— Honour's Broad Stone—a glorious name, of which the spot is well worthy.

After a bathe in the Lahn the next morning, we pulled down to Coblentz, shot the bridge, and continued our course to Neuwied, a town surrounded by tobacco plantations, and whose inhabitants are a harmonious (?) mixture of Jews, Protestants, Herrn-huters, and Catholics. We set the Professor ashore for provender, and created much excitement among a herd of boys, just let out of school, many of whom we found to be the sons of Englishmen.

Numbers of the steamers that ply on the Rhine, both passenger boats and tugs, have for some days past recognised us as they either meet or overtake us. There is always an exchange of civilities between our coxswain and the man at the helm, and frequently a sympathizing hat or handkerchief is waved from the deck of the steamer, or sometimes we are greeted with the cheers of some excited Englishman, who may be seen rushing about the deck to obtain a full view of our boat.

Made a long halt upon an island just below Andernach, and feeling, after our meal, rather romantically inclined (much in the same state of mind, perhaps, as the cockney who declared that this part of the Rhine was *so rural!*) indulged in a chapter or two of Longfellow's *Hyperion*, beginning with the story of Pelznickel and the Legend of the Christ of Andernach.

In the evening, as we floated past Remagen and St. Apollonarisberg, we gradually came in full view of the glorious old Siebengebirge, with the ruins of Rolandseck and the island of Nonnenworth, we could not refrain from another chapter of *Hyperion;* and had we landed on the pretty little island, should have, no doubt, taken it as a matter of course if we had met either Paul Fleming or the disconsolate Roland himself.

At Königswinter our costume much surprised the fashionables in the *salle à manger*, and we overheard them making remarks on the colour of our hands and faces (which long ere this had assumed a tint not easy to describe—a copper hue with a mixture of olive green being the nearest approach to it), and the extremely wild appearance we had generally.

We persisted on putting the boat into a small garden in front of the hotel, and this quite upset the equanimity of the accomplished waiter, who, however, finding that we were determined, tacked about, and became remarkably civil. 'My gentlemen, going downwards?' said he; 'at which time will you supper?' and later in the evening, 'My gentlemen, good night!' In fact, 'my gentlemen' formed the commencement of all his remarks.

On our ascending the Drachenfels, we discovered, to our disgust, that the ruin which 'castles the crag' is half covered with stupid remarks, or the names of those who have thus attempted to gain immortality at a cheap rate. Amongst others we noticed the name of our quondam friend Mr. Briggs, though we were happy to find but few English names there. A fellow actually came up to us with a pot of red paint and a brush, asking us to bedaub the walls in a similar manner; and a most quaint expression of wonder and surprise played in his features as the Doctor seriously commenced decorating the man's jacket with the half-ground mixture of vermilion and oil.

The race of

> Peasant girls with deep blue eyes,
> And hands which offer early flowers,

must have died out since the time of *Childe Harold*, for we were unable to discover any, although we made a severe search for the same.

We stopped at Bonn to dine, but having unfortunately dropped into the largest hotel in the place, we were obliged to sit out a long *table-d'hôte*, though not altogether devoid of interest, for we very much annoyed an Englishman by recognising him as such. Towards evening we reached Cologne, for we had only floated down from Bonn, much to the Doctor's delight, for he greatly preferred lying at full-length in the bows to pulling, were it ever so gently. We shot the bridge of boats at Cologne in our usual manner, but were then puzzled where to find a landing place.

'I see a jolly place,' cries the Captain ; 'just in there, under the Hôtel de Belle Vue ; let's run in ashore.' But the crew seemed inclined to mutiny, and the Captain, making a virtue of necessity, said : 'Very well, down stream, if you like, then ; you wont find a landing-place for the next mile and a half, I know.'

Fortunately there were no pebbles on board the boat, or he might have been tempted to throw down the yoke lines and commence this interesting pastime once more ; but, as usual, he soon recovered, and when we turned the boat round, with her nose up stream (having discovered no landing place), laid hold of an oar and pulled back to Deutz.

There was a fashionable concert going on in the gardens of the Hôtel de Belle Vue, but on our arrival, the audience forsook the music, and came to see the new wonder. We had a recurrence of the same scene as we had been accustomed to meet on our arrival at any large town,—when we have landed and set the boat ashore, there we must inevitably remain at the water's edge, until the crowd have satisfied themselves that we are human —that it is really a boat, or whatever doubts beyond these may cross their minds.

In the Cathedral, the following day, a gentleman came up and asked the Captain, if we were not the three English gentlemen who had arrived yesterday in the mail boat. He told us that he had heard of us for the last week, and had been expecting us every day. He asked us the particulars of our expedition, and afterwards we discovered for what reason he was so minute in his inquiries, for the next number of the *Cologne Gazette* contained an account of us, of which the following is a literal translation.

'In the French and German papers is to be found a most wonderful account of an English boat voyage, the performers of which, now in Cologne find themselves. We are in a position thereupon to give certain particulars. The three gentlemen from England, who for the last fourteen days have on the Rhine in their light craft travelled, have not in it, as has been falsely reported, from London over the sea, but per steam-boat and railway to Paris travelled. Here first begun the boat-voyage. In going up the Seine, they made one and a half, (and not as has been said) three leagues in the

Ship! — Duck!

London. John W. Parker & Son, West Strand. 1854.

hour. On the Canal of Burgundy (which joins together the Seine and Saône), and on that of the Rhône to Rhine (which connects the Saône, by means of Doubs and Ill, with the Rhine). Where there was no stream their course was quicker, but the many sluices which they had to pass hindered them very much. The most dangerous part of the voyage was from Hüningen to Strasburg, and the most arduous from Mannheim to Heidelberg up the Neckar. Their in-London-out-of-American-fir-wood-built boat, is twenty-one feet long, three broad, and weighs only one hundred and eighty pounds.'

The proprietor of the Prinz Carl Hotel, where we were stopping, showed us this paragraph in the morning, in high glee, and we found that during the day the news had circulated pretty freely, for there was an immense crowd collected to see us leave the bridge on our way to the railway station, some half a mile down the river.

We had held a council of war, and had come to the conclusion that we had better not carry out our original intention of going to Rotterdam by water, for, independently of the lack of interest on the river below Cologne, the Professor's time was nearly out, it being necessary for him to return to England before the end of another week; we determined, therefore, on sending the boat by rail to Ghent, and thence taking canal through West Flanders.

We were unable during our stay at Cologne to make up the full number (though we counted a good many) of the abominations of the city. Coleridge says—

> I counted two and seventy stenches,
> All well defined, and several stinks.

But in his time most likely they had not the fountains or streams of *Eau de Cologne* running in the streets.

I here append the legend connected with the Cathedral for the benefit of the unlearned.

Once upon a time there was a poor man, who having committed some very wicked deed, was condemned to death; but it was granted to him that if he could produce something very extraordinary he might perhaps be pardoned. He went away, as might have been supposed, very disconsolate, puzzling his brain to find out some wonderful novelty. Now it would seem that this man was of an architectural turn of mind, for one day he was seen on the banks of the river, scratching his head with one hand (which has, I believe, since

THE CATHEDRAL.

become a necessary process in the parturition of a novel idea), and with the other running out on the sand a rough outline of an ecclesiastical building on a large scale, in fact, 'an unstudied idea of a something,' as one of our English architects would have said. He finished his work, and retreating a few paces to observe the general effect, began to admire the beauty of his own imagination, when an old 'respectably dressed' gentleman tapped him on the shoulder, and whispered 'Strasburg.'

He therefore obliterated his drawing and commenced afresh, and when he had nearly finished this attempt, the old gentleman said, 'Yes—Amiens.' And so on for two or three more; at last the old fellow said: 'Lend me your cane,' and going to work, quickly run out a design for a cathedral, with which the poor man was enraptured. 'Now, then,' said the old gentleman, 'I have no particular wish to injure *you*, but I will give you this plan on one condition,—that he who first enters this building shall be condemned to perdition.' When, therefore, the choir of the Cathedral was completed, and about to be consecrated, the poor man, who of course had long ago been pardoned, went and informed the authorities of the nature of his compact. And they putting their heads together, very wisely as they thought, sent a dog into the Cathedral first, supposing that thus they would avoid the terms of the unpleasant affair.

But the Devil, for my reader has already recognised him in the respectable old gentleman, again called upon the poor man, and told him because he was thus cheated, he would take good care that the building should never be finished. And so it remains to this day incomplete.

But it must be said, nevertheless, that a great deal has been done towards the work these last few years, the nave being now open, and one of the transepts in a fair way of being finished in a year or two.

CHAPTER XIII.

BELGIUM—THE CUSTOM HOUSE.

In the different parts of Flanders you have distinct climates. Her people, who in her various provinces are marked with the races of Spain, of Holland, and of France, differ not more widely than the temperature of her several quarters ; she has her swampy flat towns intersected with canals, adapted to her peculiar constitution; she has her rarified and salubrious air of Brussels ; while in her southern parts she has her mountainous localities, differing in nothing from the invigorating breezes of Switzerland ....
There are certain laws and regulations touching foreigners, most necessary to know, since an infringement of them, either through ignorance or neglect, may bring the Englishman into trouble, and cause him annoyances, most desirable to be avoided.—Addison's *Handbook for Belgium*.

THE journey from Cologne to Ghent was by no means a pleasant one. The jarring motion of a railway carriage, after the easy swing of the boat, was very disagreeable, and beyond this there was the prospect of our having soon to end the expedition altogether. Soon we were to separate and settle down to quiet work again, though no doubt with increased health and spirits, and with a host of pleasant reflections, sufficient at least to last out the winter.

We had packed the boat up very carefully, and having lashed the oars to the thwarts, placed her upon a truck laden with wool sacks that was going all the way to Ghent. Sending her in this way we avoided the heavy charges we should otherwise have incurred had we hired a truck for the purpose, as we had been compelled to do from London to Newhaven. But the carriage of the boat the whole way from Cologne to Ghent, a distance of one hundred and ninety miles, only cost us three francs, while on the English line we paid something over one pound for sixty miles, and that was considered a bargain. As she was of course to travel by the *petite vitesse*, we had time to visit one or two places on our way. But it is quite needless to describe the Belgian towns, since they must be already so well known by numbers of our own countrymen, and are now most of them brought by the aid of steamboat and railway within such an easy distance of London, that it would take less time to get to Brussels, for instance, than it would to reach Cornwall.

We were well known by this time, it would seem, for only the day after we came to Ghent the following paragraph appeared in one of the papers.

'Nous mentionions la semaine dernière, le voyage entrepris par trois Anglais par la France, dans un petit bateau. L'équipage est à Gand, et il attend le bateau qui doit arriver par le chemin de fer de Cologne, l'intention de ces messieurs étant d'aller à Ostende par le canal et de là en Angleterre.

'Ils commencèrent leur voyage *par le Havre*, etants arrivés de l'Angleterre avec leur embarcation par le bateau à vapeur. Du Havre, ils remontèrent la Seine jusqu'à Paris, et de là, la Marne et les autres rivières, jusqu'au Rhin. Ces messieurs voyagent pour leur agrément, et *un d'eux est officier de la marine royale anglaise.*'

Among the very many interesting objects in this once rich and luxurious city, there is one which deserves especial notice—the *Béguinage*, a place of great extent, with streets, squares, and gates, surrounded by a wall and moat. Many of the sisters (who live in separate houses, none being bound by any vow, though it is their boast that no one has ever been known to quit the order having once entered it), are persons of wealth and rank. Their occupation is to attend the sick in the *Béguinage*, or to go out into the town as nurses. This is their principal establishment in Belgium, amounting to more than six hundred inmates. What a fine thing it would be for society in England (to say nothing of the benefit the poor would derive from such an institution) if a few of those unfortunates who have nothing else to do but talk about other people's affairs, could be placed in such an establishment as this!

A custom, which is said to have been handed down from the fifteenth century, when the number of weavers in Ghent amounted to forty thousand, still exists in the town. A bell was rung at morning, noon and evening to summon the weavers to their work and meals; while it tolled, the drawbridges over the canals could not be raised for the passage of vessels, and other persons were even enjoined not to go out into the streets for fear of interrupting the vast stream of population; while children were carefully kept within doors, lest they should be trodden under foot by the passing multitude.

GHENT. 135

One evening we attended a concert, which was given in the open air by the various musical societies of Ghent, which number as many as fourteen, vocal and instrumental. Some of these clubs are confined solely to the operatives, others are composed of ' respectable tradesmen,' and others of private gentlemen. The music on the whole was good.

On the arrival of the boat, we discovered that she had been roughly handled at Verviers by the douaniers of the Belgian frontier. The canvas was *torn* off, and the oars were knocking about in the boat. The covering was also plumbed, and we were informed that before proceeding any further we must declare the value of the boat, &c.; so we set a negociant or broker to work, and were then told that we must either pay duty on the boat (one hundred francs) or else send her on to Ostend by rail at once, declaring her 'in transit' through the country. But we were not very willing to accept either of these propositions, and stood out against the former vigorously, the Captain showing them that it was really contrary to the law, at least in spirit, for 'gentlemen travelling in their own carriages pay no duty for carriages or horses,' and our boat was our private carriage: but they could not or would not see it in this light.

At length, after two hours' fruitless talking with them, they said if we chose to have the boat *plumbed,* we might pay the one hundred francs then, and they should be returned to us at Ostend when we left the country; and perceiving that better terms than these were hopeless, we accepted them. We could not agree, however, to either of the propositions made by one of the wise douaniers; first that we should have the boat to take by canal and send on the oars and rudder by rail (what mode of progression we should have adopted under these circumstances it would be difficult to discover), or secondly, that the large leaden seals of about three pounds weight should be affixed to the blades of the oars in case we took them with us. By a great deal of entreaty we at last persuaded them to tie the lead seals on to the thwarts, and next we had a large document given us describing the boat in full—the number of *tons!* the depth in the water and height out of the water, the length and breadth, the description of cargo and number of crew, the oars, sculls, boathook, rudder, and *rudder strings!* It was also stated on the paper that we were allowed six days to take the boat from Ghent to Ostend, but if we wished a prolongation of time at Bruges, we should receive the grant on application to the proper authorities there.

All this so enraged the Captain, that in the spirit of John Bull bullied and writing to the *Times*, he forthwith indited a letter to the Editor of the *Independance Belge*, at Brussels, relating all our late annoyances, and adding, that in the year 1849 he wished to bring a mahogany outrigger pair-oar into the country, as he was going to reside for a couple of months at Bruges, with a fellow-collegian. This boat was at first prohibited altogether, but eventually she was allowed to be landed, after a deposit of two hundred and fifty francs were laid as a security that she should leave the country in two months time; and he concluded by saying that he had this year, with two of his friends, passed through France and Germany without difficulty, but rather had met with great civility and attention at Paris, Dijon, Besançon, Strasburg, Mannheim, Mayence, Coblentz, and Cologne; in fact, that in every town we had visited we had been received as gentlemen; in Belgium we had been treated as smugglers, or at least had been put on the same level as bargees. All this was too strong for them; they refused to publish it.

But we had not done with the douaniers yet.

The moment we had cleared the railway station, just immediately outside the gates, we were stopped again; a 'town duty' was demanded, though we only had to cross the road to put the boat into the canal. The toll was trifling, but the delay occasioned in waiting for the papers, &c., was very annoying, especially as we had spent all the morning in debating the former affair.

Pulling through Ghent by the various canals, we came before long upon a large piece of timber, spiked with iron, which lay right across the canal, and being fastened both ends to the sides of the canal, most effectually impeded our progress.

'Confound it,' said the Doctor, 'it's my belief we never shall get away from this place.'

'Don't be in a hurry,' replied the Professor, whose powers of endurance under exasperating influences was very great; 'I'll jump ashore and see what is to be done.' And suiting the action to the words he walked back a quarter of a mile, and at length found the official whose duty it was to keep guard over the said log of timber. He told us that the hour for passing it had gone by, and that we must wait till the following morning, for it was only opened for the passage of barges and boats four times during the day.

However, by the application of the silver key, the obstacle which thus had intruded itself in our path was eventually removed, and we pulled away from Ghent, by no means sorry to leave the town where we had met with so much annoyance. The fact is, we had been spoiled in France and on the Rhine, for they made so much of us at any place at which we rested, and we became everywhere such popular characters, that we were not at all prepared for the great let down we underwent on our entry into Belgium.

This evening we reached Lovendeghem, a small village on the banks of the canal, where we tried in vain during the best part of an hour to find lodgings for the night. The people at the *Estaminets* demanded our passports; said they never took in strangers, and the like; and we were preparing for a bivouac, when we learnt that there was an Englishman residing in the village, who, fortunately for us, at that moment made his appearance, and kindly offered us beds for the night, which we gladly accepted, for there was every appearance of rain coming on.

The next day we pulled on to Bloemendael (the vale of flowers), but we could discover no vale (the country being a dead flat), and very few flowers.

We should not have been at all sorry if there had been more of the latter than there actually were, for the scent arising from the flax which lay rotting in the adjoining fields was anything but agreeable.

An easy pull during a lovely afternoon brought us to Bruges, and the wild music of the *carillon* in the Tour des Halles being wafted across the Minnewater by the evening breeze, fell in subdued reverberations on our ears as we approached the Porte St. Katherine.

> In the ancient town of Bruges,
> In the quaint old Flemish city,
> As the evening shades descended,
> Low and loud and sweetly blended,
> Low at times, and loud at times,
> Changing like a poet's rhymes,
> Rang the beautiful wild chimes
> From the belfry in the market
> Of the ancient town of Bruges.

Our fame had preceded us, for we were asked by several persons, as soon as we came to a halt, if we were not the three English gentlemen who had lately descended the Rhine in our little boat.

We arrived here only just in time to put the Professor into the train for Ostend—to wish him good-bye and a pleasant passage to England, and then the Doctor and Captain, having first found a convenient spot at which to keep the boat, made off for the Hotel de la Fleur de Blé, where we took up our quarters for a few days.

We discovered the reason that our voyage was already so well known in Bruges, for one of the daily journals, *L'Impartial*, had given a full description of our proceedings, the details of which were premised by the following words:—

'Parmi les eccentricités britannique les plus curieuses, la plus singulière, sans contredit, est celle de trois officiers de Marine, Anglais, qui ont entrepris de promener leur yacht—pavillon maritime— dans toute l'Europe centrale. Voici quelques détails sur la première partie de leur voyage.'

'Our three originals,' it goes on to say, 'have pulled up the Seine and other rivers in France always in their small boat,' &c. Making so complete a jumble of several different accounts, that it would be difficult for any one to discover from this where we *had* been.

In a day or two we applied at the Bureau des Douanes for a prolongation of our stay at Bruges, but we were referred to the Prefecteur d'Arrondissement, and having explained the case to him, modestly requested his permission to remain with the boat for one week longer.

'One week!' said he; 'what do you want here all that time? What are you going to do?'

The Captain replied, 'We have friends in the town, and—'

'Oh! I can't help that; I'll give you two days more; but as to a week, that's quite out of the question.'

We could not refrain from a laugh when it came to this.

'Here's a go, Bill!" said the Doctor.

'Never mind, old boy,' replied the Captain; 'we'll get the other side of him yet. Au revoir, Monsieur le Prefecteur d'Arrondissement, au revoir.'

And we left him not a little astonished at our merriment.

Throughout Belgium many quaint and primitive notions prevail, some few of which are well worthy of notice from their extreme simplicity.

Formerly, as everybody knows, it was the custom to hang street-lamps in a very different manner to that in which they are now arranged. A wire chain was suspended across the street, and the lamp hung from the centre, being raised or lowered by means of a rope passing over a couple of pulleys, the end of the rope being confined in a

SCHEEPSDAEL.

small box affixed to the side of one of the adjacent houses. This box was kept locked; the lamp lighter only having access thereto; although in many towns on the Continent this custom still prevails, it is one that can hardly be recommended, seeing that on a moderate calculation it would take a man a quarter of an hour to light and arrange each lamp.

At the basin of the Bruges canal a bell is suspended from one of the walls hard by, for the purpose of calling the workmen from dinner, &c.; the bell-rope, hanging down by the side of the wall, enters a small box of the above description; and the end of the rope is carefully enclosed and locked up every time the bell is used. It had never struck the ingenious designer of this elegant piece of mechanism that it would be possible to ring the bell (as is actually the case) by simply taking hold of the rope above the box.

We had only been in Bruges a day or two, when we were served with a summons to attend at a certain hour at the Palais de Justice, for we had unwittingly omitted to pay the enormous toll of twopence-halfpenny in passing under a wooden bridge which crosses the canal at Scheepsdael, a small village near the town. It was a new idea to us certainly, to be called upon to pay for passing under a bridge, but as we were liable to be fined five and twenty francs for having omitted to pay the toll, we thought the best plan would be to apply at once to a Juge des Tribunaux, who having heard our explanation of the affair, politely told us that he would settle everything for us without our appearance in court.

Several of the Brugeois expressed much curiosity about the boat, and one more plucky than the rest not only ventured to get into her, but actually essayed to pull—the poor man was obliged to go home and take to bed after about twenty minutes' work. Others, however, having heard that one of their countrymen had ventured, were desirous of following the example, and three much bolder than the rest undertook to pull to Ostend, a distance of thirteen miles; and what is more, they accomplished it.

While at Ostend we took a cruise in the 'Undine' a little way out to sea, the crowds of visitors, who were either bathing or taking their constitutional walk on the Digue, showing a good deal of interest in our proceedings, as the little boat now rose on the crest of a wave, or was nearly lost sight of in the trough between two.

THE DIGUE. 145

The Digue is a very pleasant place for a walk, quite equal to the Parade at Brighton, and free from the dust, though it hardly deserves the description that has been given of it, saying that 'it is certainly the finest walk in Europe; the only thing indeed throughout the world with which it can be compared being the much talked of walls of China. Like these it stands high; the sea at low water is forty-feet below you, the moat on the other equally beneath you; a gentle sloping declivity on either side serves as a fortification on the one hand and a barrier against the waves on the other.'

Here also at Ostend we witnessed a fish auction, which was being carried on in the Dutch fashion; the auctioneer *descends* in his prices, the first man that bids becoming the purchaser. This seems after all to be the fairest method; for you do not stand a chance of being run up by hired bidders or of being tempted by ordinary competition.

CHAPTER XIV.

CONCLUSION.

> Of this allow,
> If ever you have spent time worse ere now,
> If never yet, that Time himself doth say,
> He wishes earnestly you never may.
> *Winter's Tale.*

DURING our stay at Ostend, we made application for the one hundred francs deposit, which we were told could not possibly be paid us until the 'Undine' had left the port on board of the steamer; but by the kind assistance of Mr. St. Amour and a Belgian naval officer, we eventually prevailed on the Chef de Bureau des Douanes to give us permission to keep the boat still longer in the country. We therefore cut away the lead seals, from the boat, paid the fifteen francs duty they demanded, and then returned to Bruges.

The Captain having made arrangements to remain still longer on the Continent, set to work to build an outrigger *funny* or wager boat. He experienced no small difficulty at first in getting the proper materials for his work, but eventually, through the assistance of Mynheer Hoelvoet, he procured a few planks of Memel timber in the place of American yellow pine, and forthwith laid down the keel.

While she was in process of building, we required the assistance of one or two natives to hold on the plankings which were being fitted to the sides of the boat. We soon found, however, that they rather hindered us by their frequent irrelevant suggestions, and the many better modes of boat-building than that which we had adopted.

'Watchte bitje, Mynheer! Me go you tell in few time; you put so kleine bitje hoot* thereup—ja! 'tis schneller and sehr gemaklyk.'†

'Yes, yes, I see it is *gemaklyk* enough—pak‡ dat—nein—die anderen seite—so 'tis wohl.'

'Voilà! 'tis all gedone. All right, eh, Mynheer?'

After a fortnight's labour the funny was completed. The manner in which she answered our expectations being sufficiently detailed in the fol-

---

* Wood. † Easy. ‡ Take.

lowing letter to the Bruges paper. I will only add that in England, the price of such a boat (the materials of which, in Belgium, cost £3 10s.) would have been £20 at least.

Monsieur l'Editeur *de l'Impartial de Bruges.*

J'ai été hier témoin d'un charmant et curieux spectacle sur le canal d'Ostende à Bruges. C'était la mise à flot d'un joli et mignon bateau, de forme bizarre, auquel en Angleterre on donne bien justement le nom de *suicide*, et qui a été construit par M. H—— infatigable et intrépide canotier, qui a su aller de Londres à Cologne, toujours par eau. Parti du Havre, il a remonté la Seine, le Canal de la Marne, et de là a passé dans le Rhin ; ensuite il a descendu ce fleuve de Strasbourg à Cologne, toujours dans son léger et joli petit bateau, qui glisse sur l'eau comme un ramier. Mons. H—— avait eu la bonté de m'inviter pour assister avec quelques amis à l'inauguration de *son suicide*. Je me trouve donc hier à 11 heures du matin sur le bord du canal, lorsque Mons. H—— arriva tranquillement avec son bateau *sur la tête*, comme ces jolies paysannes qui rentrent des bois un léger fagot de broussailles placé sur leur tête.

La nouveauté du spectacle avait attiré un certain nombre de curieux ; entre autres quelques jolies et espiègles dentellières, qui riaient à chaudes larmes et plaisantaient sans doute sur ce qu'elles trouvaient ridicule, parce qu'elles n'y comprenaient rien encore. Mons. H——, sans perdre sa gravité britannique, déposa son bateau avec beaucoup de précaution dans les eaux du canal, comme une tendre mère place son enfant endormi dans son berceau. Quelques instants après, Mons. H—— y était placé, prêt à s'éloigner du rivage, et les dentellières riaient de plus belle.

Il faut d'abord, Monsieur, faire la description *du suicide*. Le bateau est composé de deux planches, épaisses seulement de quelques lignes, à peu près comme on scie le bois de luxe pour l'appliquer aux meubles ; la vapeur donne à ces deux planches une forme convexe, et elles sont unies ensemble de manière à former une espèce de navette de tisserand très allongée ; quelques petits morceaux de bois servent à soutenir les parois du bateau. Le bateau est long 27 pieds, large au centre de 15 pouces, profond de 10 pouces, et il pèse en totalité 15 kilos.* Au centre du bateau est reservé

---

* That is, about thirty-two pounds.

un petit espace carré où se place le rameur, accroupi plutôt qu'assis; tout le reste du bateau est couvert par une légère toile de coton vernie, pour empêcher que l'eau ne remplisse l'embarcation, *qui, en voguant est presque toujours couverte par l'eau*, à l'exception du centre. Deux petits bras en fer servent à soutenir les rames, et les deux extrémités du bateau, garnies de fer, ne sont profondes que de deux pouces, et elles sont si étroites qu'elles peuvent percer l'eau avec une vélocité de 12 *milles anglaises à l'heure* (4 *lieues*). Mons. H——— s'éloigna donc de la rive avec beaucoup de précaution, se courba sur ses rames, et le voila parti comme une flèche glissant sur l'eau. A une certaine distance on ne voyait plus le bateau, mais on aurait dit, un homme assis tranquillement sur l'eau, s'amusant à manier une paire de rames; on voyait seulement devant lui le petit drapeau britannique placé à l'avant, agité par la brise, et qu'on aurait pu prendre pour une légère hirondelle folâtrant devant Mons. H——— pour lui montrer son chemin.

J'ai dit en commençant que le nom de *suicide* est justement donné en Angleterre à ce genre de bateaux. On en voit très souvent sur la Tamise, *et surtout à Greenwich, où ils font le passe-*

UN *cramp*. 151

temps favori des étudiants. Mais pour se risquer dans ces périlleux bateaux, il faut d'abord être très fort rameur, savoir bien nager, et être bon equilibriste, car il suffit d'un petit mouvement un peu brusque, d'un *cramp** (faux coup de rame) ou le passage d'un bateau à vapeur, pour que l'on se trouve tout à coup renversé dans l'eau.

Dans la Tamise l'on voit tres souvent plusieurs de ces dangereux *suicides* renversés par déplacement et l'agitation de l'eau, causés par le passage d'un bateau à vapeur. Alors les personnes qui les montent, nagent tranquillement en ramenant leur embarcation jusqu'au rivage, la remettent debout et recommencent leur périlleux exercise.

Mons. H—— m'a dit qu'il pouvait eviter l'ennui de payer le péage des ponts et la perte du temps aux écluses ; le moyen est bien simple ; il prend le bateau, le place sur la tête, et fait route par terre ; c'est le renouvellement du tour que jadis Jason et les Argonautes jouèrent au roi de Colchis, qui les poursuivait après qu'ils eurent conquis la fameuse toison d'or ; seulement il y a cette différence, que les Argonautes trainèrent les bateaux après eux à travers l'Asie Mineure, pour echapper au roi, pen-

---

* Which being interpreted, signifieth 'catching a crab.'

dant que Mons. H——, pour eviter les *gabeloux*, met son bateau sur sa tête, et cela sans sortir de la légalité.   Agréez, etc.,

S. DE CANDIA.

This beat everything in fine poetic flow of language combined with correctness of detail, that it had hitherto been our good fortune to meet with. It had been said in a German paper in regard to our cruise in the 'Undine':—'Seit 14 Tagen fuhren sie rheinab und fielen durch ihren hellblauen Auzug, die Englische Flagge und den eleganten nachen von Hüningen bis Köln viefach auf.' —'In fourteen days they have descended the Rhine from Hüningen to Cologne, calling forth the admiration of all beholders, on account of their light blue costume, their pretty English flag, and the elegance of their bark.' We had also figured in one of the French papers, near St. Jean de l'Osne, as different characters in *Telemaque*. But this letter far surpassed all the rest.

In fact the *funny* created quite a sensation at Bruges. It was not long before the *intrépide et infatigable canotier* was addressed in public as Monsieur le Chef des Regates; in virtue of which title he was enabled to meet his former friend,

CHEF DES REGATES. 153

le Prefecteur d'Arrondissement, on equal ground, and inform him that the 'Undine' had returned to Bruges.

Soon afterwards the Doctor left for England— the funny was hoisted up into one of the stables of the Hôtel de la Fleur de Blé, under the care of the civil proprietor, Monsieur Mees-Garnot, and the pair-oar being similarly disposed of, was left 'in ordinary' for the winter.

Thus ended our cruise in the ' Undine,' an excursion which had been to us agreeable in the extreme. The ease and freedom of our peculiar mode of travelling were very great. The utter independence throughout such a voyage, and the entire absence of the restraint which is incidental, more or less, upon any other means of locomotion, would have required more detailed notice here, had they not been already so ably set forth in another work.

During six weeks and a half we had travelled over one thousand miles of country; our total expenditure from London, through France, Germany, and Belgium, till we reached Ostend, amounted only to £15 each, including the carriage of the boat from London to Paris, and also from Cologne to Ghent, no small item in our expenses.

It has been hinted, since our return, that a similar excursion might be made along the rivers and canals in England for a proportionate sum of money. Perhaps it could; though the Captain doubts it much. The only attempt he has heard of, is that of a pair-oar some time in the last century. An account of this trip was given to the public under the title:—'A Very Merry Wherry Excursion from York to London, sometimes Perilous, sometimes Querulous.' But, even adopting this economic mode of travelling, the expenses would necessarily be much greater in England than on the Continent.

The Captain is aware that even in London one may live luxuriously at a cheap rate. You can have a dinner of soup, meat, and vegetables, drink a glass of spirit and water, smoke a cigar, and go to a theatre afterwards, for the small sum of sixpence. It is possible. Go to the Whitechapel soup kitchen; true, you will find the pewter soup plates screwed, and the ladles chained to the tables; but you receive a bason of soup, with a piece of meat and a potato therein, for threepence. You then walk to Holborn (we will say nothing of the cost of shoe-leather), where you purchase one pennyworth of gin and help yourself to cold water

CONCLUSION. 155

from a large tub, and then, after smoking your penny cigar, you adjourn (if you choose) to a neighbouring *Gaff*,* for admittance to which you also pay one penny.

Let me assure my readers, if it be at all necessary, that ours was a very different style of living to this, otherwise we should not have been fit for much work, and it is not to be denied that we had our share of this, especially while we were going 'up stream.'

But let me hasten my conclusion ere I completely wear out the patience of my reader, should he, perchance, have come thus far.

As I said in commencing, this little book is the log of 'our cruise' only; should the sketches and etchings please (as they can hardly fail to do, proceeding from the hands of talented, though they be amateur, artists), and the journal help to pass away a weary hour, the object of the writer is accomplished.

Should this unvarnished account of ' Our Cruise in the Undine' induce other crews to undertake a similar expedition, we heartily wish them (as they cannot fail to reap) as much pleasure, both in

---

* Vide *London Labour and London Poor*.—MAYHEW.

anticipation and retrospection, as much profit both to mind and body, as it has been our good fortune to have enjoyed.

And for our little book, it is but a bubble on the stream, perhaps faintly resembling in its nature the capricious water-nymph herself; and 'although it may catch the sunshine for a moment (as we are sanguine enough to hope it may) yet it will soon float down the swift-rushing current, and be seen—no more.'

NEW BOOKS & NEW EDITIONS,

PUBLISHED BY

John W. Parker and Son, West Strand.

Annotated Edition of the English Poets.
By R Bell. In Monthly Volumes, Foolscap Octavo, 2s. 6d. cloth, each:—

Poems of the Earl of Surrey, of Minor Contemporaneous Poets, and of Sackville, Lord Buckhurst; with Critical Notes and Biographical Memoirs. 2s. 6d.

Poetical Works of John Dryden, Vol. I., with Memoir containing New Facts, and Original Letters of the Poet. 2s. 6d.

Dryden's Poetical Works. Vol. II. on the 2nd March.

A Year with the Turks. By Warington Smyth, M.A. Crown Octavo.

Of the Plurality of Worlds. An Essay. 8s.

The Mediterranean Sea. A Memoir, Physical, Historical, and Nautical. By Admiral Smyth, D.C.L., Foreign Secretary of the Royal Society. Octavo.

The Cloister Life of the Emperor Charles the Fifth. By William Stirling, M.P. Third Edition, considerably enlarged. 8s.

The Little Duke; or, Richard the Fearless. By the Author of ' The Heir of Redclyffe.' With Illustrations by J. B. 5s. 6d.

The Heir of Redclyffe. Fourth and cheaper Edition. Two volumes, 10s.

Hypatia; or, New Foes with an Old Face. By Charles Kingsley, Rector of Eversley. Two Volumes, Post Octavo. 18s.

The Youth and Womanhood of Helen Tyrrell. By the Author of ' Brampton Rectory.' 6s.

Brampton Rectory; or, the Lesson of Life. Second Edition. 8s. 6d.

Compton Merivale: another Leaf from the Lesson of Life. By the same Author. 8s. 6d.

Yeast: a Problem. By C. KINGSLEY, Rector of Eversley. Cheaper Edition. 5s.

Digby Grand: an Autobiography. By G. J. WHYTE MELVILLE. Two Volumes. 18s.

The Upper Ten Thousand. Sketches of American Society. By a NEW YORKER. 5s.

Jesuit Executorship; or, Passages in the Life of a Seceder from Romanism. Two Volumes. 18s.

The Merchant and the Friar; or, Truths and Fictions of the Middle Ages. By Sir F. PALGRAVE. Second Edition. 3s.

Bacon's Essays; with the Colours of Good and Evil. Revised from the early copies, with the References and Notes by T. MARKBY, M.A. Cloth. 1s. 6d.

Bacon's Advancement of Learning. Revised from the early copies, with the References, an Index, and Notes by T. MARKBY, M.A. Cloth. 2s.

Principles of Imitative Art. Four Lectures delivered before the Oxford Art Society. By GEORGE BUTLER, M.A., late Fellow of Exeter College. 6s.

Three Weeks in Palestine and Lebanon. By a CLERGYMAN. Thirteenth and Cheaper Edition. 2s.

Meliora; or, Better Times to Come. Edited by VISCOUNT INGESTRE. Two Series. 5s. each.

The Philosophy of Living. By HERBERT MAYO, M.D. Cheaper Edition, with Additions. 5s.

Lives of Eminent Christians. By RICHARD B. HONE, M.A., Archdeacon of Worcester. Four Volumes, with Portraits. 4s. 6d. each.

Bishop Jeremy Taylor; his Predecessors, Contemporaries, and Successors; a Biography. By R. A. WILLMOTT, Incumbent of Bearwood. Second Edition. 5s.

PUBLISHED BY JOHN W. PARKER AND SON. 3

Travels in the Track of the Ten Thousand
Greeks; a Geographical and Descriptive Account of the
Expedition of Cyrus. By W. F. AINSWORTH. 7s. 6d.

Gazpacho; or, Summer Months in Spain.
By W. G. CLARK, M.A., Fellow of Trinity College,
Cambridge. Cheaper Edition. 5s.

Auvergne, Piedmont, and Savoy: a Summer
Ramble. By C. R. WELD. 8s. 6d.

Schiller's Poems, Complete. Translated by
EDGAR ALFRED BOWRING. 6s.

Summer Time in the Country. By Rev. R.
A. WILLMOTT. Second Edition. 5s.

The Saint's Tragedy. By C. KINGSLEY,
Rector of Eversley. Cheaper Edition. 2s.

Goethe's Opinions on the World, Mankind,
Literature, Science, and Art. 3s. 6d.

Introductory Lectures delivered at Queen's
College, London. 5s.

Crusaders; Scenes, Events, and Characters
from the Times of the Crusades. By T. KEIGHTLEY. 7s.

The Lord and the Vassal; a Familiar Ex-
position of the Feudal System. 2s.

French Revolution; its Causes and Conse-
quences. By F. M. ROWAN. 3s. 6d.

Labaume's History of Napoleon's Invasion
of Russia. 2s. 6d.

Historical Sketch of the British Army.
By G. R. GLEIG, M.A., Chaplain-General to the Forces.
3s. 6d.

Family History of England. By the same
Author. Cheaper Edition. Three Volumes. 10s. 6d.

Minerals and their Uses; in a Series of
Letters to a Lady. By J. R. JACKSON, F.R.S. 7s. 6d.

NEW BOOKS AND NEW EDITIONS.

Familiar History of Birds. By the late Dr. STANLEY, Bishop of Norwich. Fifth Edition. 5s.

Leaves from the Note-Book of a Naturalist. By W. J. BRODERIP, F.R.S. Post 8vo. 10s. 6d.

The Comets: a Descriptive Treatise; with a Condensed Account of Modern Discoveries, and a Table of all Calculated Comets. By J. RUSSELL HIND, Foreign Secretary of the Astronomical Society. 5s. 6d.

An Astronomical Vocabulary; being an explanation of all Terms in Use amongst Astronomers. By J. RUSSELL HIND. 1s. 6d.

Shipwrecks of the Royal Navy. Compiled principally from Official Documents. By W. O. S. GILLY. With a Preface by Dr. GILLY. Second Edition. 7s. 6d.

The Earth and Man; or, Physical Geography in its Relation to the History of Mankind. By PROFESSOR GUYOT. Slightly abridged, with Corrections and Notes. 2s. 6d.

Indications of the Creator — Theological Extracts from Dr. Whewell's History and Philosophy of Inductive Sciences. 5s. 6d.

Bible Maps; an Historical and Descriptive Atlas of Scripture Geography. With copious Index. By W. HUGHES. Cheaper Edition, in cloth, and coloured. 5s.

Manual of Geographical Science. PART THE FIRST, 10s. 6d. containing—

MATHEMATICAL GEOGRAPHY. By Rev. M. O'BRIEN.

PHYSICAL GEOGRAPHY. By D. T. ANSTED, M.A., F.R.S.

CHARTOGRAPHY. By J. R. JACKSON, F.R.S., &c.

THEORY OF DESCRIPTION AND GEOGRAPHICAL TERMINOLOGY. By Rev. C. G. NICOLAY.

Atlas of Physical and Historical Geography. Engraved by J. W. LOWRY, under the direction of Professor ANSTED and Rev. C. G. NICOLAY. 5s.

LONDON: JOHN W. PARKER & SON, WEST STRAND.